M000041601

JAR: A Vessel in the
Hands of the Potter

JAR: A Vessel in the Hands of the Potter

The First Twenty Years in the Life
of Jesse Alan Rivers

JESSE ALAN RIVERS

foreword by Jedd Medefind

RESOURCE *Publications* • Eugene, Oregon

JAR: A VESSEL IN THE HANDS OF THE POTTER
The First Twenty Years in the Life of Jesse Alan Rivers

The Holy Bible, New International Version®, NIV® Copyright© 1973,
1978, 1984, 2011 by Biblica, Inc.™ Used by permission. All rights reserved
worldwide.

Resource Publications
An Imprint of Wipf and Stock Publishers
199 W. 8th Ave., Suite 3
Eugene, OR 97401

www.wipfandstock.com

PAPERBACK ISBN: 978-1-7252-8415-9
HARDCOVER ISBN: 978-1-7252-8416-6
EBOOK ISBN: 978-1-7252-8417-3

Manufactured in the U.S.A.   11/03/20

For you, yes YOU, the precious child who has been or feels unlovable, invisible, overlooked, unwanted, abused, abandoned, rejected, isolated, and/or unvalued. Please read these pages, encountering the true love and words of the Potter for YOU!

For you, yes YOU, the advocate and champion for precious children. Your long, tedious, and never-ending work of fighting to see justice for the voiceless, the down trodden, the broken, and vulnerable has not gone unnoticed. Maybe, just maybe, this world will be blind to the gem that you are, and will not be worthy of your presence, but know that God sees it all, and sees you as a beautiful diamond, shining brilliantly.

For you, yes YOU, who have been generous and good to me. Sometimes my busy-ness and travels have made me less than present, and maybe even forgetful of the gratitude you deserve. God sees you and has a great "Thank You!" waiting for you, in His timing! I also thank you, from the depths of my heart!

Contents

Contents

Acknowledgments

There is a long list of people who have been influential in my life, and also in making the publication of this memoir possible. The first I shall thank though, is God Almighty. *Lord, without You, I could never have done this. Thank You for loving me, saving me, redeeming me, and for granting me the blessings of this great life! Please take this testimony and use it for Your glory! Capture hearts, change lives, and encourage and inspire a multitude of people to know just how awesome, amazing, and loving of a Potter You truly are! Amen!*

I have an incredible amount of gratitude to extend to my spiritual father, co-laborer, and dear friend . . . Pastor Mike Holland. Thank you for loving me with the love of a spiritual father. Thank you for your patience and faithfulness to challenge, encourage, and help move me forward. Though you have known my greatest weaknesses, you have seen my heart and love for God, and you have loved me for the man of God that I am; regardless of my faults, failures, and weaknesses. Your insistent belief that God wants to use my life, and your encouragement for me, have had an eternal impact for the glory of God. There are treasures in heaven stored up for you! Thank you again!

Many thanks also go to Grace Holland. 'Grandma' Grace (Mike's mother) was the first person to read through this manuscript to edit it in its early skeleton stage! Thank you, Grace, for the hours of work you invested in making corrections and suggestions to get me moving forward, that have undoubtedly made this book more cohesive, less repetitive, and easier for others to read and understand. It is better because of you! Thank you!

I also would like to thank 'Shannon and Willy'! Your love for the Lord, and your surrender to allow God to use your lives to impact my heart and life for His glory, cause more gratitude within me than I can really express! Thank you, Shannon, for leading me to Jesus, and showing me how to live and love a bit more like Jesus. Thank you, Willy, for having long talks with me; sitting in the rocking chairs in the living room, and walks and talks in the berry fields as well, throughout my teen years. Those are very dear and special memories that I hold on to. Thank you both for allowing the Potter to use you both as vessels to reach out to this hurt, broken, smelly little boy from just down the street. Many of the spiritual disciplines in my life today have been greatly influenced and nurtured because of your great example, love, and investment in me. I am certain that there are treasures stored up in heaven for both of you! Thank you both again!

I also desire to thank my dear friend, Faith. Many, many thanks to you for your persistent prayer support and love, over the years. You are my longest prayer partner and encourager in my life, and are an amazing blessing to me! You have been a motherly voice of wisdom and encouragement, and your prayer support and communications with me have been a constant blessing to me. Thank you for showing me of God's great love! Hugs, blessings, and love . . . and many thanks!

With great gratitude, I also want to thank Marilyn and Chuck Morris! Though they have no desire for recognition, I still want to give a huge "Thank You!" to you both for your part in enabling for this memoir to be placed into the hands of many. Thank you for your time and great investments, edits, suggestions, and great wisdom to help me get this, my first book, in a finalized form to be published! Your extensive help and thorough attention to details have made this book even better! Thank you both, again!

A special "Thank you!" to Ralph, a man who was required to sit with me for many hours throughout my adolescence, and who taught me to play chess and cribbage. Ralph, you invested in my life, even if it was partly your job. You went above and beyond and helped a lot of my healing process in life. Thank you for caring about me beyond a paycheck; truly seeking to love and help me well. God has seen your work, and is pleased!

A "Thank you!" to the staff at Wipf and Stock Publishers (and Resource Publications), is also important here, as they have worked hard to help me get this book off the press. Thank you for the patience and good communication that you have maintained for and with me. Here's to hoping for a long and successful working relationship.

There have also been so many other people who have been influential in my first twenty years of life, as well as others who have helped me along this path to complete and print this memoir; and for my omission of recognition I greatly apologize. However, to each of you who know the impact and influence you have had in my life, please take joy in knowing that God also knows and He does not forget! He remembers all acts of love and kindness, and will rightly reward them. Thank you to each of you who go unnamed here! You are not unnamed before God!

Foreword

The most profound question in all the world takes just three letters to write: *Why?* That is not merely *a* question. It is *the* question.

Why? Why so much pain? Why such sorrow and loss? Why neglect and abuse? Why do we even exist at all?

The first twenty years of Jesse Rivers' life carries more of these *Why*'s than one could count. The twists and turns of his stranger-than-fiction story include pain beyond what any child should bear.

Yet, marvelously, they do not lead merely to a crumpled, "Why?"

Rather, Jesse's account makes a bold claim, one every bit as profound as that age-old question. No, this story does not attempt to solve every riddle or answer every objection. Nor does it pretend that tragedies are easily forgotten or that wounds don't leave scars. Yet even so, Jesse's claim is able to stand toe to toe with the question. It looks *"Why?"* in the eye without flinching.

Here is Jesse's claim, woven through every twist of darkness and light in the pages ahead:

The place of our greatest hurt can become the place of God's greatest work—first in us, and then through us.

Yes, our world is profoundly broken, as Jesse recounts with heartbreaking honesty. Yes, the sorrow of the human soul is sometimes beyond description. But for those with eyes to see, God is yet at work. What others intended for evil, He can redeem. If this is so, pain is not only something we may endure. It is something that can, quite literally, be smelted by Love into unparalleled good.

To be sure, this is an audacious claim. One could raise a thousand objections. But it is backed by good evidence for those willing to consider it. This includes the richest stories and deepest truths of Scripture . . . the lives of God's people all throughout history . . . and, most of all, the gospel itself. Thanks to this book, it includes the remarkable account of Jesse Alan Rivers as well.

Having walked as friends with Jesse for a decade now, I've seen that firsthand. Certainly, Jesse would remind us that he is still growing, that healing is a lifelong process, and that none of us will ever be entirely whole until God makes all things new.

But every time we're together, I find myself marveling at the man Jesse is today. Somehow, all that he experienced over so many years of mistreatment has not yielded what one would expect—rage or resentment or a lifeless soul. Rather, Jesse glows with bright eyes, a grateful heart, and an earnest desire to serve God and neighbor.

Years ago, Jesse and I spent a day exploring in Yosemite National Park. At every curve in the trail or bend in the river, he'd spot some new beauty, a fresh glory, to point out and rejoice in. *The way the dark green of oak leaves contrasted with the gold of dry grass. The rainbow-blaze of a waterfall shot through with sunlight. Even a single flower or chirping bird.*

As Jesse explained during our drive home, he saw in each beauty, large or small, an expression of "the 101 million ways God says 'I love you,' to each of us each day."

For Jesse, this unbounded gratitude was not merely an attempt to "look on the bright side." Rather, it was the fruit of eyes that have been baptized with hope. As Jesus might put it, Jesse has "eyes to see." And so he lives with a heart of confidence that—even amidst many yet-unanswered questions of *why?*—a loving Father is at work for the good of His children, able to use even unspeakable hurt for unimaginable good, just as this book describes.

On that day in Yosemite, I quietly prayed that God would grow my eyes and heart to be more like Jesse's. I'm still learning. But I sense God is indeed granting that request—little by little, in part simply as I get to spend time with Jesse and hear him share his story and all that he sees.

I'm so glad that you now have that privilege, too—getting to spend time with Jesse and hear him tell his story and what he sees. As you do, I trust that God will grow your eyes and heart to be more like Jesse's as well.

JEDD MEDEFIND
July 28, 2020

Preface

Greetings and blessings! I want to thank each of you for taking the time to read this small glimpse into my first twenty years of life. It is my sincere hope that it will be a blessing to you, as well as a challenge for you. If you know God, as the Potter that He is, may you value His fingerprints on and in your life even more. If you do not yet know the Potter, may His hands and fingers work to use this book as a crafting tool, to bring you to knowledge and into relationship with Him. May each of you be impacted in a beautiful and positive way, all for the glory of God!

As you turn the pages of this book, you will quickly realize that I have lived quite a dramatic and full life, even just in the first twenty years! Those years were very traumatic and yet transformative, and offered me great revelation into hardships and challenges, as well as beauty and blessings of life. Jesus Christ is my Savior and my Lord. I believe in God, and if that is offensive, you may want to put this book down. I am unashamedly certain to the core of my being that God exists, and also of His great love for me. I know that I could not have lived my first twenty years of life without Him!

All ages and experiences that I share will be from my best recollection. However, exact dates given are correctly dated. Most names used in my testimony will each be a pseudonym to protect the person's privacy and identity.

Throughout this book, I will be vulnerable and descriptive about the people and situations I have encountered, exactly as I recall them. It will not be an easy read, nor do I suggest it be read by children, so please prayerfully proceed. My purpose in sharing so openly is in no way to be disparaging toward those who have hurt me, nor is it for your pity. I share so openly to enable you to see what God has rescued me from, and to see how powerful and awesome the Potter is! Please do not judge me nor the others from my past, as we each are still a work in progress . . . jars in the hands of the Potter . . . and I am well aware that I still have many faults, failures, and blemishes to overcome. God is continuing to work on me! As you read this memoir, may you sense the Potter's hands and love!

Most of us are familiar with the basics of what a jar is. Each jar is a uniquely shaped vessel. Until most recently, with today's technology and production advancements, most jars were molded and crafted by the hands of a potter. Jars come in many shapes, sizes, and colors. Each jar has a very specific purpose: a decorative piece in a home, a vessel to transport or hold items, an object of practice and perfection for honing the potter's skill; to name just a few. A jar's value and purpose are given by the potter and/or owner. Its beauty comes from the imagination and artistic creation of the potter. Its durability comes from the material which the potter uses, and its shape and size are also determined by the potter.

I am certain that I am a JAR in the hands of the great Potter, God Almighty. Within the pages of this book, may you see how God, the Potter and Creator, has been molding and making me a vessel for His purpose and glory; as so eloquently stated in Romans 9:21. I also know that the Potter still has a lot of work to do, on and in this JAR, before I am brought to His desired finish. It is my prayer though, that you will also begin to recognize the fingerprints of the Potter even more in your own life. The Potter is at work!

The following is my personal testimony of the Potter's majestic and redemptive hand upon my life, throughout my first twenty years!

Names & Descriptions

Shelly: Shelly is the biological mother. She suffered significant abuse in her childhood and throughout her some of her adulthood as well. Though she passed on the abuse to her three biological children, I am continuing to pray for God's redemptive and restorative work to take place in her life, that she will (or has) come to truly know and follow Jesus Christ as her personal Savior and Lord.

Paul: Paul was the biological father. He was accused by Shelly of not wanting children. According to Shelly, Paul left my life while she was pregnant with me. I never met or knew him, and while I was in college I was notified that he had passed away. Though I never could verify the reason why he had left Shelly and his biological children, I pray that he knew Jesus and is now with the Potter.

Stefan: Stefan is the step-father. He also suffered significant abuse throughout his childhood and adulthood, some of which I even witnessed when I was a child. Stefan was a very angry man. He often turned his aggression on to me and the biological sisters. I continue to pray for healing for him, that he would know Jesus, and have his past, present, and future redeemed by God. May the Potter mold and shape him for His glory.

Anne: Anne is the oldest biological sister. She suffered considerable brain damage from extensive abuse as a baby and throughout her infancy. She greatly lacked in common sense, but had a great heart. I pray for her that she would really know Jesus and the power of the healing hand of the great Potter.

Kate: Kate is the other biological sister, and the middle child. In my time of knowing Kate, she possessed a sharp mind to manipulate and control situations, very much like Shelly. However, she seemed less motivated to hurt people. I pray that God, the Potter, has molded and shaped Kate to really know Him.

Shannon and Willy: Shannon and Willy are the Christian couple who introduced me to Jesus. I view them as fingerprints of God on my life. They introduced me to God's pure and faithful love, and they reflected it very well to me. They also put up with me being in their home for several of my adolescent years. God has great rewards for them, for their patience and grace with me.

Julie: Julie was a young model who worked at a mental institute/psychiatric ward. Julie was used by the Potter to reveal my sanity and innocence in a very crazy situation, which you shall read about, as you continue. Julie was another fingerprint of God in my life.

Faith: Faith has been a beautiful and positive mother-like influence throughout my life. I met her at church when I was in my early teens, and I became friends with her and her family. She remains an incredible encouragement and support for me. I praise God for the beautiful fingerprint of God that Faith has been in my life.

Chapter 1

In the Beginning . . .

My introduction to this world began on a cold and blustery winter night, in the city of Lewiston, Maine. I was born at 11:30pm, on November 27th, 1978. The weather outside was quite chilly (a brutal ten degrees Fahrenheit), but the situation I was born into was even more frigid. I was born not only to people in financial hardship, but also as an unwanted child. I was not the only unwanted child though, as I was the third child (first boy) born to the biological mother and biological father, Shelly and Paul.

Shelly and Paul seemed to share a mutual mindset that children were a hassle, a problem, and too much responsibility. When Paul learned that Shelly was pregnant with me, he was so upset about having yet another child that he just packed up and walked out. At least, that is how Shelly explained it. It is hard to know the truth though, because Shelly was quite prone to lie, deceive, manipulate, and to control things. She always strove to paint herself in a good light, and to make things work out for her favor. For whatever reason, though, Paul exited the picture.

Shelly was not happy that Paul had left her, and she wanted to win him back. Right from my birth I was exposed to her deceit and manipulation. I believe that she figured, if she named me after Paul, being his first and only son, he would naturally come running back. She seemed to have thought that a father, having a son who bore his name, would feel a great sense of pride and connectedness to the child, which would cause Paul to return home. Therefore, Shelly named me ____ ____ ____ Junior; thereby giving me Paul's full name and making me a junior (Jr.). However, Shelly's attempt to control the situation and win Paul back failed. It appears as if he did not take pride in having a son that bore his name, as he had left and was to never return.

Though Paul had withdrawn himself from the picture, while I was still in the womb, his name that I now bore was not so quickly gone. I had an ugly curse placed upon my life; being named after a man who could not, or did not want to, be a part of my life. My identity was connected with one who had abandoned me, before I was even born. Shelly's master plan of manipulation to win Paul back had failed. So, while his name stuck with me for a long time, Paul did not.

God, the Potter, in His infinite wisdom, placed a fingerprint on my life from the day I was born though. No one ever called me by the name that I had been given at birth. Everyone simply knew me as "J.R."—the initials used to abbreviate *Junior*. If you were to venture with me back to Maine, and if people there still remember me, you would hear them all call me, "J.R." I see this nickname as the first of many fingerprints of God, the Potter, upon my life.

After Paul's departure, Shelly blamed me and sought to punish me. At least, that is my understanding for why she abused me so intensely. Time and time again, she manipulated and controlled situations to make my life miserable. She seemed bent on punishing me and removing pleasure from my life. Praise the Potter that He had enabled me to see the beauty in life, even while suffering the great pain and deprivation that Shelly so regularly caused me.

While I was still an infant, Shelly decided to marry another man; Stefan. Stefan was over six feet tall and quite strong, due to being raised on a farm. Stefan was a man of a similar mindset and perspective about children as Shelly. In fact, he was even more emphatic that he did not want children, and he was always reminding me and the two biological sisters, whom I will refer to as Anne and Kate, that he was not our father.

Stefan's attitude was not so much to manipulate or control us, as Shelly strived so much to do, but rather, he just wanted to have absolutely nothing to do with us. It seemed that kids were not a consideration for him, even in marriage. He made sure to tell us often that we were not his kids, and that we would never have anything that belonged to him. He was a man of explosive anger at times, and his anger, height, and strength worked together to almost kill the three of us children on several occasions. Praise God for His angels and protective hand to save and guard our lives. Each time the hand and fingerprints of God were upon us, to enable us to endure what no child should ever have to endure.

For the first thirteen years of my life, I endured significant physical, sexual, verbal, mental, and emotional abuse. I also often suffered specific abuse directed at me, as Shelly intentionally deprived me and strove to punish me and inflict pain. Most of the abuse I suffered will not be articulated in this book though, because it was far more intense than most people could imagine, handle, or believe. The sexual abuse that I personally went through was committed by numerous individuals, males and females; some were relatives, others were not, throughout my first thirteen years of life. I am not looking for this book to be a pity party for me, so I will be reserved in how much I share of specific abuse.

The abuse in the home setting was not always focused on me exclusively, but also on Anne and Kate. Amazingly, despite all the pain, abuse, and suffering, God had placed in me a deep value and love for life. I could daily see and feel beauty and goodness all around me, though we were in the throes of immense and ugly abuse.

For the first few years of my life, due to living in an economically challenging situation, we lived in government run, low-income apartments throughout the twin cities of Maine, known as Auburn and Lewiston. We would live in those apartment complexes only during the fall, winter, and spring because this was the time of year when the weather often reached frigid and unbearable temperatures, and we needed a warm and solid roof over our heads.

During at least one of the summers of those first few years, we lived in a big yellow school bus that Stefan drove throughout the school year. Not needing to drive the bus during the summer, he would park it on his father's farm property, and that is where we would sleep and live throughout the summer. I'm not sure how many can say that they have lived in a big yellow school bus, or would even want to, but I really enjoyed changing seats to sleep each night. God had put a fingerprint of an adventurer upon my life. I must admit though, that I did not enjoy the constant challenge of wetting the seats and the subsequent beatings I received for not being able to control my bladder. Of course, living in a school bus also presented other challenges such as showering, eating, etc. Despite these challenges, those summer memories from my first few years are precious to me. I remember that living on the bus brought some relief from the intensity of abuse. The summers also brought heat and sun, which seemed to give me hope and joy.

Stefan's father owned a large farm with literally hundreds of acres of land. It was a sprawling property, where there was an apple orchard, cider mill, a huge barn, a farm house, chicken coop, double garage with a smaller garage right next to it, sprawling hay fields, potato fields, other fields filled with various produce, hills, rippling brooks, and dense forests all around. Each of these places offered lots of space for escaping the abuse, and for living out great childhood adventures.

I remember though, the constant gnawing fear and anxiety of someone being displeased with me, whether with or without cause, and then violating me with their words, bodies, and/or actions, or just depriving me of something. However, I also remember, on numerous occasions, hiding in the hay in the barn, talking with the cows and farm animals, getting intentionally lost in the forest, shimmying up between the two garages to just lay on the flat roof of the smaller one, or just lying in one of the many fields for hours to escape the abuse from Shelly and Stefan, as well as others. Despite much pain and abuse in these early years, God used the time of summers on the farm to imprint upon my heart and mind a deep appreciation of life and beauty, as well as offering me all the exciting adventures of exploring nature on the property, including the neighbors' properties. I can recall to this day the sense I had, this great feeling of winning despite the pain and trials I suffered.

I almost always seemed able to produce a smile. I have never seen myself as a victim, but rather as a victor; victorious over the abuses, injustices, and challenges of life.

One adventure, that I only participated in just a few times, was to lay next to the road in the ditch and act as if I was unconscious. I did this half way up the big hill, on which the farm sits. I would wait for cars to come speeding down the big hill, or to come barreling around the big curve in the road below, flop myself down in the ditch, and wait to hear the screeching tires. People were concerned, as I had intentionally sprawled myself out to look hurt or dead, and I really liked the attention. There was a both a bolt of excitement and fear that would shoot through me, in the same moment. I would be sure to disappear in the hay field as soon as I heard the brakes though! This continued only until one vehicle pulled into the farm property and reported my actions to Shelly. That was one beating that I probably deserved! It was a short-lived adventure, but I'll never forget it.

From as young as I can remember, I worked long days on the farm with Stefan. I learned how to work hard, and how to keep the farm functioning; including the cider mill, tractors, and running the chain saw. There was always plenty to do, from stacking cords of wood, to filling the basement with chopped fire-wood, digging potatoes, tending to the agriculture, helping with the haying, shoveling dung, retrieving eggs from the henhouse, milking the cows, and caring for the farm animals. In an odd way, work became yet another way to escape abuse. Though I still received beatings from Stefan while working on the farm, they were less frequent and far less intense. Sometimes Stefan even showed pride in my strength and ability to work hard. It was these small glimpses of goodness and kindness over those years that would help me, later on in my teen years, to work through the process of genuine forgiveness for this man.

I reflect back on my years of working on the farm, and I realize that God used that time to develop my muscles and physically strengthen me. This would serve as a blessing from God that aided me in surviving several intense beatings throughout most of my childhood, and I see it as another one of the many fingerprints of the Potter on my life. I learned at a young age to appreciate the burn of muscle-building, and I learned that sometimes good things come out of hard situations. Pain had produced strength in my muscles . . . and also, in my life.

In the right seasons, I loved to escape to the wild berry patches or take refuge in an apple tree, to eat all I could before Shelly found me. Sometimes there were even crates of smashed apples, used for making cider at the cider mill, that were the pulp and left over. These crates of apple 'waste' were placed on a concrete slab on the side of the cider mill, to be given to the pigs to be able to eat. I often snuck some of these apple remains, and enjoyed them greatly! They were sweet and I understood why the pigs would like them. Unfortunately, there were often two negative consequences. One was that eating too much of anything causes pain and a negative impact on our bodies. When you are as hungry as I was, and as deprived of food, sometime self-control to know when to stop went out the door, and I would end up with a bad stomach ache. Secondly, Shelly did not want me to enjoy food or, for that matter, life, so my indulgence also often led to beatings, if she found out. So, though these sweet and forbidden tastes sometimes were great relief from the deprivation of flavor and pleasure, they also came with a risk of pain.

My constant fear of Shelly was strong enough to keep me from asking for food, though my stomach was almost constantly crying out to be fed. Due to the deprivation of food, to this day my stomach rumbles and makes a lot of noise, though now I can eat as healthy, or unhealthy, as I want to. Sometimes those apples and berries were just enough to appease my hunger briefly, but it would quickly return.

Another fingerprint of God on my life was, and is, my appreciation for the gift of life. Despite being born into such a hard situation—the youngest of three, born into a poor biological line, being unwanted, suffering intense abuse, and living with people who did not want or love their children . . . I loved life! God gave me eyes to see, ears to hear, and a positive perspective to appreciate the beauty of the world all around me. While I may repeat this truth a lot, I am, to this day, completely amazed at how the Potter has created and protected me to be one who truly enjoys the gift of life.

I remember as a young child I always loved seeing other people smile. It made me happy just knowing that others were happy and smiling, and this made me long and hope that I too would one day be free to be happy and smile. Praise God that I smile a lot now! Seeing other families, where parents really loved their kids and gave good gifts to their children, made my heart hopeful and happy as well.

While I was still very young, Stefan moved us out of the low-income apartments, as well as away from the school bus, and moved us into a three-story apartment building which he had purchased in the middle of the city of Auburn. The apartment building was located on the left-hand side of the road, halfway up a small hill, but at that time to me it seemed like a mountain. The building that Stefan bought was at 24 Vine Street, Auburn, Maine, 04210. Different challenges were about to be encountered in this new residence.

In this new location I was introduced to a new 'companion' which continued for many years to plague my life. This 'companion' was the distinct feeling that I was an unwanted and unlovable person. It did not help matters that Shelly forced me to sleep on the second floor of the apartment building all by myself, while everyone else slept and lived on the first floor. The seclusion continuously served as a painful indication that I was unwanted and unlovable. These are feelings I have had to guard myself from throughout my life. Yet now, many years later, I've learned to run into the arms of my awesome Father and Potter, God Almighty. However, as a young boy, I had no clue where to turn when I was attacked by loneliness and rejection.

Ironically, on one of my windows in the bedroom, there was a decal picture of a firefighter climbing down a ladder away from a burning building. In his strong arms, the firefighter held a little boy tightly against his chest, as he rescued him from the burning building. The firefighter's face showed great compassion for the little boy, and it was obvious that the child was treasured by the man who was rescuing him. I started yearning to have someone rescue me, someone who would hold me just like the firefighter was holding the little boy. I often dreamed of being that little boy in the man's arms, and even received comfort from such dreams. I wanted to believe in my little heart, though much of the world around me seemed to say differently, that I could be loved and valued for exactly the little boy who I was.

Much of what I encountered in early life worked in opposition to me truly feeling valued and loved. One of my earliest memories, when I was about four years old, in the three-story apartment, is that I was sitting near the fireplace on the first floor playing with some Lego building blocks, which someone outside the family had just given me. Maine can get extremely cold, and I have always loved heat, so I was seated near the fireplace. As I sat playing with my little Lego blocks, Shelly walked by and unknowingly stepped on one of them. She immediately struck me with her fist, yelled at me, and grabbed all my new Lego blocks and threw them into the fire. This shocked me at first. However, thinking back on the event, I believe it prepared me for the ongoing abusive and selfish things Shelly would end up doing not only to me, but to Anne and Kate as well, throughout the next decade.

I remember, in that moment, wanting to jump into the fire to rescue my Lego blocks. I felt bad for them. Even if I never got to play with them ever again, I wanted to be compassionate like the fire-fighter in the decal on my bedroom window. I felt bad for my blocks, not selfishly, but because God had already put His fingerprints on my heart to be compassionate and caring of others and of things around me. It may seem silly to some, but I really felt bad for them.

Another vivid memory from the three-story apartment was of me sleeping alone on the second floor. At night I would sneak into the hall, to turn on the light. In my little boy imagination, this light seemed to be possessed somehow because it was always flickering. Now, as an adult, I'm aware it was probably the result of an electrical wiring issue, but as a little boy I believed it was possessed by a nice ghost who would protect me. I don't recall where or how I learned of ghosts, but I felt peace and comfort from having the light to turn on during the dark, lonely nights. I also remember carrying on conversations with the light (not that it ever responded) and it helped me feel safe as I would fall asleep.

It was not unusual for Shelly and Stefan to lock Anne, Kate and me out of the house. We would then walk the streets, play in the back yard, or go to a nearby park for hours. Sunday mornings, we would hear loud music coming from a nearby church, Court Street Baptist Church, and it was as if the music was luring us to come. Anne, Kate, and I often walked up the hill and a few blocks to the right, on Sunday mornings, to attend the church. It was situated just above the Auburn courthouse, and so was aptly named. I see this church as yet another of the many fingerprints of God on my life, that He led us to there.

Although it was for the loud music, free yummy food, and an atmosphere of lots of smiling and happy people that initially led us to the church, God miraculously used this time to imprint some of His songs and His Word in my heart. Although I was unaware of it at the time, this is when God really started drawing me to Himself. Some people say hindsight is 20/20. I say that hindsight is often what brings me to my knees in praise to God for the wonderful, beautiful, and mysterious ways in which He works to draw His children and creation to Himself! In that church, the first song I ever heard was "Freely, Freely." This song imbedded itself deeply within my heart and mind, and, though I did not totally understand it at the time, it started causing me to focus on and believe in God. It planted a seed of the Gospel message within me, and started me wishing for a God who would rescue and free me.

When Shelly and Stefan did not resort to just locking us out of the house, they would often get us out of their hair by sending us to a married couple across the road, or another couple who lived just up the road. The couple who lived across the road were rather wealthy and arrogant. They were verbally abusive towards us kids, as they constantly told us how dirty, smelly, and gross we were. There was a tangible sense of condemnation; that they thought they were much better than us.

The other couple, who lived up the road, was by no means wealthy nor condemning, but they were physically and sexually abusive toward the three of us. We knew them as Vons and Rosie, but later we learned that these were not their real names. They disappeared suddenly at one point, and we were to never see nor hear of them again.

When I was still five years old, on October 27th, 1984, something horrific happened in a home nearby to where I was living, that had a traumatic effect on me as a young child, received international news attention, and still causes me great grief in my heart to this day. Just a couple of miles from where I lived, John Lane and his long-time girlfriend, Cynthia Palmer, the biological mother of Angela Palmer, a four-year old girl who was my dear friend, put Angela inside their oven, after physically beating her, closed the oven, and turned it on. Then they continued to hold the door closed on this tortured and dying child! John believed that Angela was possessed by the devil, and claimed to be trying to get rid of the devil. Even as I sit here typing these words, remembering what they did, I am choking back tears, as I think about the vile and senseless death of my friend. Sin is so ugly and stupid! Sin is godlessness. Praise God, He is not like that! Praise God that He has good and perfect gifts for His children (James 1:17 NIV), and He has a plan and purpose for us as well! His purpose is *not* to harm us, but rather to love and bless us! May more parents be like Him, loving and blessing their children! May I, one day, get to be a father like Him.

Chapter 2

Moving to be Meaner

Shortly after my dear friend, Angela, had been murdered by her parents, Stefan moved us away from the center of the city into a run-down, dumpy trailer. The trailer was located at the end of a long dirt road on the outskirts of the very small town of Mechanic Falls. I had often wondered why Stefan sold the huge three-story apartment building in the middle of the city for the trashy trailer. My only conclusion was that he must have purchased the land along with the trailer, because there were acres and acres of forest all around us. This massive forest provided total seclusion, which meant no accountability from neighbors and people in the public eye, for how Shelly and Stefan treated us. Unfortunately, for Anne, Kate and me, that was an invitation for increased abuse and neglect from both Shelly and Stefan.

When we first moved into the trailer, our water came from an old well dug behind the trailer. There were many times throughout the year, including in the middle of the bitter cold Maine winter, when I was forced to go draw water from the well to either flush the toilets or so we could boil the water to cook, drink, wash dishes, or take baths. In the well, there was a long, thick, white, braided rope tied to a pail. I would let the pail down into the water at the bottom of the well and draw it back up once it was full. If the well had frozen over, I would try to break the ice, to avoid another beating, but many times with no success. When I was successful at drawing water, I would untie the rope and lug the five-gallon bucketful of water into the house, and then repeat the process several times! Although it was very heavy, it also helped my young body to develop more strength. When I was around ten years old Stefan finally paid for an artesian well to be drilled and then we had the luxury of reliable running water, hot and cold, connected to a new trailer.

Shelly was always a bit eccentric in her tastes, and would paint the wall and floors of the trailer fluorescent brown, green, and orange. Her clothes also reflected her eccentric nature, and were often embarrassing to see her wearing. She never seemed to mind or notice though. I am not sure if it was just a difference of preference and perspective, or results of the brain damage that she suffered from the abuse she had received as a child. It also may have been a strange attempt to receive attention.

Due to the poor situation of the home setting in which we lived, the dumpy trailer only had two bedrooms. The master bedroom was obviously for Shelly and Stefan. The other bedroom, at the other end of the trailer, was shared by Anne and Kate. I was left with a metal spring cot up against the wall of the small living room. Not only was it uncomfortable, but just breathing or turning over made the bed squeak. That annoying noise often resulted in beatings from Shelly or Stefan.

In addition to the regular creaking and squeaking of the metal spring cot, there was also the fact that I intentionally banged my head repetitively down onto the edge of the cot. Night after night, I would slide up to the end of the cot and bang my forehead down on the metal end for long periods of time, often leaving an open gash in my forehead. The constant banging upset not only Stefan, but also Shelly, Anne, and Kate, and led to many beatings.

While it might sound strange, at this point in my young life this felt like one of the few things that I was actually able to control. I did not want to make people mad, but there was the overwhelming need to make it through the abuse and to have some sort of control over something. The intense exposure to sexual abuse, the gut-wrenching pain from physical beatings, and the trauma of knowing that my friend Angela had been burnt alive all contributed to me sensing a desperate need to bang my head. In a peculiar way, my head-banging was a soother for me. It somehow made me feel better, as it released my anger and frustration, and made me feel more stable. It may sound strange to many, but this became a source of comfort for me as it provided calm, peace, and power in the middle of the hell and pain of all the abuse.

Although this behavior would certainly not be considered a 'normal activity' for most young boys, it is something I have now learned in my adult life that many parents with traumatized and/or abused children often deal with. In fact, head-banging is considered a common self-mutilating behavior similar to cutting, burning, or picking of skin, that is often used as a way to regulate traumatic and painful life situations. I believe the death of my friend, Angela, was probably the trigger and start to my head-banging, though there were several other traumatic influences before and after as well, and I continued banging my head late into my teen years.

As I already mentioned, Shelly desired to remove pleasure from my life as much as possible. While this worked out in almost every aspect of life, her abuse intensified when we lived in the woods. Food was regularly monitored and used to deprive/punish me. Sometimes Anne and Kate would suffer the same treatment, but most usually it would be meted out specifically to me. I remember many times I was allowed only to have puffed wheat or puffed rice for breakfast with water or powdered milk, while the others would eat sugared cereals, eggs, ham, bacon, sausage, pancakes with syrup, and all other kinds of delicious breakfast foods. Lunch and supper, when I would be given anything to eat, often consisted of liverwurst, liver, chowder, goulash, or some stew or soup, while Shelly and Stefan would eat pizza, hamburgers, steak, seafood, pasta, etc. Shelly's intentions were to give me what I did not want, and not to allow me to have anything that I would enjoy, as a way of removing pleasure and punishing me.

When Shelly knew that she and Stefan would both be at work or away, she would lock up all loose food items in a large refrigerator/freezer which she always left unplugged. She called it the dry freezer. Shelly would often observe, and sometimes even mark, amounts of contents of food items throughout the kitchen. If she found anything missing when she returned home, we would receive a very thorough beating. A sad truth is sometimes she intentionally marked items as having more than they actually had, to give herself justification and an excuse to beat and abuse us when she returned from work, and found them with less than where she had falsely marked the container.

Somehow, at a very young age, I figured out how to break into the dry freezer, and I would try to find something to eat. One of my favorite things to 'steal' was raw spaghetti. Shelly was able to mark or count most things in the freezer. However, she did not, or could not, count or measure how many strands of spaghetti were in the boxes, making it easy to steal and eat. This also worked with macaroni. (Note: I am not promoting stealing here, but I was a starving little boy trying to survive.) To this day, I think of raw spaghetti as a delicious treat. I would take a small bite of the raw spaghetti and let it sit in my mouth. The saliva would then soften it and brought forth a delicious flavor. Believe it or not, I still enjoy raw spaghetti. In fact, right now, as I write this testimony, in my bed stand there are two packages of raw spaghetti!

From as young as I can remember (maybe three years old), Shelly would go to a day-old bread store and buy the outdated bread, donuts, and pastries. This may have been because it was all she could afford, but I remember being really young and Shelly intentionally forcing me to eat an éclair that was green with mold on the inside. She saw the mold, insisted it was still good, and then took great pleasure in watching me force the gross green goo down my throat as she stood there laughing. Even today it is hard not to remember the disgusting ordeal every time I'm offered an éclair, and so it has been many years since the last éclair has entered into my mouth!

While suffering with hunger pains throughout much of my early childhood, I learned to appreciate the flavor of dog food and cat food. These were things that Shelly would not count or pay attention to, and so it was a way to fight against the yearnings and gnawing of my stomach, and to win against her abuse. Though our dogs and cats were often fed better than us kids, I do remember their ribs were also clearly visible. So I learned, early on, that a dog really can be a man's (boy's) best friend, especially when it's willing to share food with a really hungry kid. Though I do not remember most of the names of the dogs, besides Red, they were my best friends!

Bedtime was often used as another means to punish us or remove pleasure. It generally came very early each evening, unless we had been locked outside or were away visiting other people. Bedtime at our house meant no reading, writing, talking, or playing. In fact, we were not even allowed to get up to go to the bathroom, because the slightest noise could send Stefan into a fit of rage, which often led to a fierce beating. Shelly would also give us a beating if she found us doing anything, and she could give just as fierce a beating as Stefan, and often did. I have learned a lot about patience and stillness, by having to lay perfectly still for hours before finally falling asleep, to just avoid a beating.

Going to bed at such an early hour often meant that, at some point during the night, my body would need to exercise its right and freedom to rid itself of excess liquid and waste. However, because of my overriding fear of getting a beating, I would often just go right in my bed. Needless to say, this caused me to smell of urine and excretion, and also increased the problem of people not wanting to be around me. To make matters worse, my bladder and bowels were rather small because I never had to learn to 'hold it'. Therefore, I did not gain full control over my bladder and bowels until I was nineteen years old! It was a very embarrassing and long-lasting consequence of the abuse that I endured.

An added problem to the wretched stench of my body was that the privilege of bathing was not allowed to be a daily event. In fact, it was more like a rare event. This caused Anne, Kate, and me to have to go out in public smelling like urine and excretion. I remember hearing people in church and school, and out in public in general, make snide and mean comments about our smell and how dirty we were, how we did not take care of ourselves. Though I was able to put on a fake air, and acted as if it did not hurt or bother me, it felt so unfair, because in reality I have always loved water, loved to bathe, and to be clean! However, because we were not allowed to bathe often, people spoke poorly of us. There was, however, the occasional opportunity given to me specifically, to take a bath in water that Shelly had first washed in and then Stefan took his turn to wash in it. By the time it was my turn, the water was cold and had a dark gross layer of scum. It definitely was not a great privilege. Anne and Kate were more regularly allowed to shower, as the bathroom next to their room had a tub and shower in it, which I would have definitely preferred to use as well.

As another form of Shelly's manipulation, control, and a means to remove pleasure, she informed my school I was not allowed to watch any movies or videos with my class, nor go on field trips. Sometimes she even instructed the teachers not to allow me to go out for recess, and on occasion I was not allowed to participate in gym class. She also would not allow me to participate in any after-school extra-curricular activities, nor play sports or be a part of any after-school groups. I also was not allowed to have friends, at least not outside the school walls. She 'convinced' (or tried to convince) the school that she was prohibiting these activities solely for my protection, because she did not want me to get hurt. I do recall some of my teachers expressing regret to me because of these excessive regulations, and their lack of belief in Shelly's motives, but their hands were tied because Shelly was the legal guardian. So many of the joys that normal kids have in going to school were robbed from me, because of Shelly's manipulation.

My fifth-grade year was a good school year for me, though many would probably see it as one of my worst. It was while I was in fifth-grade that I learned that, if I got a detention, I would be required to stay after school, and Shelly could not stop it. I remember intentionally getting a ridiculous number of detentions in fifth grade just to give myself some relief from all the abuse at home. I would be intentionally loud, obnoxious, and disruptive, so that I would be able to enjoy the quietness and freedom I found in detention. I probably still hold the record for detentions in that school, at least for a fifth grader. It appeared that Shelly considered the detentions as yet another form of punishment, so she never punished me for getting them, except to make me walk the mile hike back to the trailer. Praise God! I had lots of strength and endurance, and I enjoyed the freedom of slowly walking back to the trailer; avoiding as much time in the abusive home situation as I could!

It is a bit ironic that my detentions were one of the biggest joys in my first thirteen years of life. Each detention offered momentary bouts of freedom from my abusive home, while also providing a safe place to do my homework and relax without having to worry about being beaten. I actually enjoyed (and still enjoy) studying, learning, and doing homework. God had blessed me at that time with a very high IQ, which Shelly could not take away from me. While she would take away all my academic awards, pile them up in a box under her bed, and then use them as fuel for bonfires, she could never take away my intelligence and the enjoyment that I received through education. In Romans 8:28 (NIV) in the Bible, it says that God works all things for good for those who love Him and are called according to His purposes, and I watched God use my detentions for my good, to bless me and help me in the midst of hard and horrible circumstances! Detentions for me were a fingerprint of God on my life!

Sometimes, as a form of control and abuse, Shelly would make Anne, Kate, and me get down on our knees and remain there for hours at a time. We had to be in an erect and full kneeling position, with our backs straight and fully extended up, with our noses placed against the wall and our hands folded behind our backs. To make matters worse, Shelly would often eat yummy food and watch television in her room, while we would remain on our knees for hours at a time, often hungry, hurting, and needing to use the bathroom. Sometimes she would come out and just hover around with a ruler or stick, ready to smack us if we flinched or tried sitting back to rest. There are many times that I remember her grabbing my ear lobe and dragging me across the room, just to move me to a different location. It was very painful! Interestingly though, these cruel acts greatly increased my tolerance for pain. Today, I now willingly bow on bended knee before God regularly, and it is with great joy and love for all the Potter has done in my life. This does not bring me pain, but rather the pleasure of adoring God Almighty.

Christmas, Thanksgiving, Easter, and birthdays were a time when Shelly would try to make herself look good to other people.

In her deceit and manipulation, when we were in front of others, we were given gifts and candy, and the holidays were made out to be a big deal. She would tell us not to eat the candy, nor open the packaging of any enclosed gifts, until we got home. However, once we got in the vehicle on the way back to the trailer, the gifts and candy were immediately taken away. Shelly would eat the candy and food, sometimes sharing with Stefan, and she would use the gifts for herself—assuming they were something she wanted. If not, she would return them for a refund. Then other times, they were given away to other kids or burned in the bonfire out behind the trailer. I always knew, as she would say, "Wait until we get home!" exactly what that meant; Shelly was going to take it away! Stefan sometime seemed uncomfortable with this practice, and I could see a bit of his heart. He wasn't all bad.

Chapter 3

Saved: Pillar #1

A few months after we moved into the run-down dumpy trailer, a Christian couple, Shannon and Willy, who lived just down the road from us, came to witness to Shelly and Stefan. Neither Shelly nor Stefan had any interest in hearing about God. Shelly's mindset of God seemed to be that He is a big, mean, angry God with a big stick in His hand, ready to beat you over the head for any thing you do wrong. Though Shelly would never allow me to do anything she thought I might be able to take pleasure in, she was more than willing to allow this Christian couple to pick the three of us children up each Sunday morning, to take us to Sunday school and church! Little did she know, and little could she or I have ever imagined, just how much pleasure and joy would, and has, come into my life because she allowed me to attend church with Shannon and Willy. Sometimes Shannon and Willy wouldn't come for us, but we would walk down the road to their house, to ask if we could go to church with them on those Sundays, and they were very often willing to take us.

Shannon ended up being my Sunday school teacher, while Anne and Kate were in another Sunday school class. Shannon is one of the best story tellers I have ever met in my life. She also is a lady of immense love, and really knows God and His heart for people. She lived out His love each week, as she and Willy sacrificed to pick up and take us three smelly and obnoxious children to church regularly, to share and show us the love of God. Shannon's ability to demonstrate and convey God's love through story-telling was very attractive to me and immediately got my attention, because I so desperately longed to be loved. Her love stories about Jesus were captivating.

Each week we met in the kitchen of the church basement for Sunday School. Shannon had an amazing ability as a story teller, and she was able to make you feel like you were a part of each story. I felt as though I was actually in a den with Daniel, while ferocious and hungry lions were growling and prowling all around us. I could feel their breath on my arms, though they were unable to touch me or Daniel, because God had shut their mouths. I looked Goliath in the eye, as I watched David hold his sling in one hand and five smooth stones in the other. I followed Moses into the Red Sea with towering walls of water rising up on each side of us, as Pharaoh and his army were charging at us from behind. I sat on the edge of a hillside overlooking a sea, as Jesus loved on the multitude around me, providing physical and spiritual nourishment. It was as if I was truly part of these and so many other Bible stories that Shannon shared week after week. Shannon also told us some cool stories about a character named Sunday School Charlie, as well. She used a flannel board to illustrate those stories, and I was always captivated by her storytelling. Yes, Shannon had an amazing ability of putting me right in the midst of every story.

Shannon would always close our Sunday school class each week with the same theme, which appeared to me to be her favorite. She always focused on Jesus Christ and His love for people. I loved hearing the hope that came from Jesus' presence in the different stories, for those living in hardship. I remember hearing about little Zacchaeus climbing up into a sycamore tree, to be able to see Jesus, and Jesus saw him! My little heart hoped and longed, that if there really was a God, that He could and would choose to see, love, and help the little unwanted boy I was too. After all, it truly felt like I had some vicious lions roaring all around me, walls of water towering around me, with an army pursuing me from behind, and a giant in front of me that wanted to kill me. I longed to be the main character of a story, where God would show up and rescue me as well! I was not looking to be the hero or rescuer in the story, but rather to be the one God loved and whom He would reach down to rescue.

One Sunday morning, when I was seven-years-old, Shannon's favorite story took on a whole new dynamic for me. It was that very morning, as Shannon was sharing about Jesus Christ's love for humans, when God became a reality to me, and no longer just the great character of a good book. I felt stirred and burdened as I had never experienced before, to accept Jesus Christ as my Savior; an opportunity which Shannon offered to everyone in the class every week. I truly sensed the hand of God upon me, impressing upon me that this message was meant for me, that I was to accept Jesus Christ as my Savior.

At the end of Sunday school class, Shannon asked if anyone wanted to accept Jesus Christ as their Savior—to be forgiven of their sins, but no one raised their hand. Shannon then closed the time in prayer and dismissed us all to go upstairs into the sanctuary for the morning church service. As all the other kids in the class dispersed to go upstairs, I stayed behind and waited for them to all leave. I remember that Shannon was still clearing off the sticky paper figures from her flannel board, from another Sunday School Charlie story. After everyone had left, I asked Shannon to tell me again about this God who could love me. How was it possible that the Creator of everything could truly love someone and something as small, dirty, smelly, and as worthless as I had started to believe, and always had been told, that I was? The next few moments would become some of the most precious of my lifetime.

I must pause here, to best prepare you to understand the major significance of that morning in the kitchen of the church basement with Shannon, as more of the home environment in which I lived must be shared. Not only was pleasure and enjoyment intentionally removed from our lives as children, but also any sense of dignity, worth, and value were stripped from us. Shelly and Stefan had always told us how dirty, ugly, gross, stupid, smelly, and worthless we were. Though this mainly took place in the home environment, many of these opinions were also experienced and felt from others at school, church, and out in public as well. The words, "I love you," were seldom shared with us. Shelly might say those words to manipulate us to do something, or to make herself appear good in the eyes of other people around us, while out in public. She also might say those words to one of us to intentionally try to hurt us or to make the other two of us jealous. However, those words seldom, if ever, were sincere or held much of any meaning. Though I longed to be loved, I understood Shelly's manipulation and control, from the earliest of ages, enough to realize her words held no weight or sincerity. Stefan, on the other hand, just didn't want us around, and continued to remind us that we were not his children! So, love was not something we experienced in the abusive home situation.

Out in public, positive affection and attention were seldom directed toward Anne, Kate, or me from anyone. As we smelled of urine and excretion, and were dirty and disheveled, we were often avoided by most people. We were also obnoxious in our attempt to receive attention . . . at least, I was! Even negative attention seemed better to me than no attention at all. We also did not know appropriate ways to interact with people, which caused others to intentionally avoid us.

That Sunday morning, as I stayed behind in the basement of the church, as a little boy who had been repeatedly abandoned, rejected, and abused in all manner and fashions, as well as told how unlovable I was, I asked Shannon to tell me again about this God who could love me. My heart's yearning to belong and my life's longing to be loved peaked, and I wanted to know if it was really true that I could be loved. In the next few minutes, as Shannon thoroughly shared of God's love for me, forgiveness of my sins, and gift of salvation for me, God placed in me the faith, trust, and acceptance to know that He could love me. Yes, even foul, dirty, stinky, unlovable, worthless little me! Though I lived in a situation very much deprived of love and acceptance, somehow Shannon (and God!) had convinced me of God's amazing and freely-given love for me. When Shannon finished explaining about God's love, my sin, His grace and forgiveness for my sinfulness, and my absolute need for Him as my Savior, she proceeded to lead me in the salvation prayer. Then and there I accepted Jesus Christ as my Savior!

In my life, there are two moments that I consider to be pillars of my faith; concrete moments that can never be taken from me, which have moved me from being someone of just blind faith to a man with certainty of God and His love for His children. Jesus Christ is the solid rock, the foundation of all that I am and all that I believe, but I know that many in society might try to dismiss this as just my own personal belief system. However, beyond just this 'belief system,' I have two pillars of my faith; tangible moments and experiences of my life that take my faith from the point of just being faith and a belief system, to being a completely certain knowledge of God! These two pillars can never be removed from me!

The first pillar of my faith occurred on that early Sunday morning, in the church basement kitchen with Shannon. It happened in that moment, as I was accepting Jesus Christ as my Savior. As I asked Jesus Christ to forgive me for my many sins, to change me and make me new, and to come into my heart, mind, and life, there was an immediate release of a dark, heavy, oppressive weight which lifted up off my body. It was like 3,000 pounds of a very dark and heavy weight lifting off my body! It started moving up from the tips of my toes and swept all the way up through my body. As this dark, heavy, oppressive weight was leaving up from my toes, feet, legs, to my chest, off my shoulders, and leaving above my head, my body was being refilled with an unbelievable electricity, light, peace, and vibrancy beyond description. People talk about 'cloud nine,' well I'm sure that I hit clouds nine, ten, and eleven! It was an amazing and unforgettable moment in my life that can never be disproved or taken away (even with all the psychological evaluations and explanations). This moment and experience was the first pillar of my faith! It was a supernatural and amazing event, and I knew with unshakeable certainty that God really did/does love me and came to save even me! The Potter is a Rescuer!

After accepting God's gift of salvation and grace in my life that morning, I went upstairs with Shannon to attend the morning church service, that took place in the sanctuary after Sunday School. During the announcement time of the service, Shannon stood up and shared with the congregation that I had accepted Jesus Christ as my Savior. Suddenly, people in the congregation were extending hugs to me, and welcoming me into the family of God. While the hugs were nice, appreciated, and something I had desperately desired for so long, they were nothing compared to the supernatural, intimate hug and eternal relationship of love that I had just entered into directly with God in that basement. I was still on clouds nine, ten, and eleven, from Jesus' hug and salvation!

While Anne and Kate stood back and watched as I received those hugs, I knew what they must be feeling. They longed to be loved, hugged, wanted, and needed just as I had. When we returned to church the following Sunday, it came as no surprise to me when both Anne and Kate proclaimed that they too had accepted Jesus as their Savior. I understood these confessions were made so they could receive physical hugs from the members of the congregation. My heart was grieved greatly though, as I have wondered if they had missed out on the eternal hug I received from Jesus Christ as my Savior. That was, and is, the very best hug ever! Only the Potter knows though, and they are in His hands.

After receiving the gift of salvation from Jesus Christ, there were many changes in my life, which were definitely not of my own doing, and many of God's fingerprints and His work in my life became evident to others as well. Unfortunately, those changes were not apparent in the lives of Anne or Kate. I continue praying that a seed has been planted, and that one day they have come to or shall also know the precious love and transforming hands of the mighty and marvelous Potter! That is my prayer!

Chapter 4

First Report and First Prayer

Accepting Jesus Christ as my personal Savior did not miraculously change everything in my life. In fact, within a few months of the time I had accepted Jesus into my life, I experienced another extremely painful beating, when Stefan came home from work, one early morning, in a deep rage. Stefan now worked third shift, late nights, in a warehouse, working maintenance. He was often angered to the point of being in a rage, and this morning was one of those times. Just looking into the eyes of Stefan, as he was in a rage, was more than enough confirmation that you should get away from him. It was such a horrific look that it made me feel paralyzed and incapable to move at all.

To explain rage well, I am going to use another word here that most would not normally relate to anger. 'Drunk' is actually a word that refers to a person being completely under the influence and control of something else. People can be drunk on pride, power, possessions, sex, alcohol, drugs, and a whole lot of other things as well. To be drunk is to have lost complete control of oneself to something else. I believe that rage can best be defined as the condition or state of a person who is completely under the control of anger, or drunk on anger. Unfortunately, Stefan went into fits of rage often, and each time provided another opportunity for God to place His fingerprints on my life. I truly believe that I am alive today solely because God's angels were intervening many times when I should have died. Yet, sometimes after an intense beating, when Stefan was worried about inflicting permanent damage on me, I would see a look of remorse and sadness in his eyes. Stefan is a human who has erred, but also has a heart and emotions. I pray for him still, to have victory over this problem of being drunk on anger, his fits of rage!

On that particular early morning, when Stefan came into the trailer in a rage, I was asleep on the metal spring cot that they had given me, placed against the living room wall. Stefan jerked me up off the cot and threw me back down onto it. However, he was so enraged and out of control that he missed his mark. As he threw me back down, I landed on the edge of the metal spring cot. My ribcage and armpit caught on the metal springs that stuck out from the edge of the cot, and I crashed and crumpled onto the floor. The metal springs had torn into my side, ripping off the skin of my ribs and arm pit. I curled up on the floor in pain; screaming, bleeding, and crying. Stefan immediately told me to shut-up, get up, and get ready for school. He laid out a whole line of swears at me, that shall not be repeated, and he was still quite enraged!

I don't know when this truth hit me, but there was a point in my early years of life when I came to a very important realization for survival purposes. It was never wise to speak to Stefan or Shelly when they were in a rage, though Shelly was in a rage less frequently of the two. She was more so focused on controlling and punishing me, for Paul leaving her. However, I had learned that when someone is in a rage and you talk to them, no matter what you say or how nicely you say it, it usually sets them off even more. You could say "I love you!" or "Here's a thousand dollars that I want to give you!" and it would only intensify their rage. Maybe it is not true for all who experience rage, but at least for Stefan and Shelly, it was best to be silent, and to stay as far away as possible.

Whether or not I knew better at this particular moment, as I laid on the floor, in excruciating pain, crying, and bleeding, I am uncertain. However, when Stefan ordered me to shut-up, get up, and get ready for school, my response was a whole line of curses at him, and I told him in no uncertain terms that I was not going to school. Though not terribly surprising, my response did indeed set him off even more. He came over, screaming and cursing, as he kicked me in the head and stomach with his steel-toed work boots. Then he began jumping up and down on my body, as I laid on the floor, in tons of pain, bleeding and crying. As he jumped on me, one of my hips popped out of joint. He then picked me up and threw me out on the porch, demanding that I would go to school. I just laid there on the porch, bloody, immobile, and in immense pain.

Within a couple of hours, Anne and Kate got up and got ready for school. Though I am certain that everyone in the trailer had heard the beating I took, they knew better than to get involved. It was not cowardice, but rather wisdom, that they had refrained from trying to deter Stefan from beating me. When you live in such intense abuse, there is like a sixth sense, that alerts you as to when you should intervene to help, and when it would not be wise to, at least this seemed to be the case for me. Stefan was in such a rage that, if Anne or Kate had got involved, he might have literally killed them. As Anne and Kate headed off for school, they came out to the porch and helped me down our long dirt road to the bus stop. It was extremely difficult to walk because my hip was out of joint, and I was in intense pain from the physical beating. My shirt was torn up and bloody, and my whole side and armpit were torn open. I limped, hopped, and was carried to school that day.

When Anne, Kate, and I got to school that morning, my teacher, a very nice lady, quickly noticed my blood-stained shirt, my wounds, and my inability to walk correctly. Immediately, she sent me first to the nurse, and then to visit with the guidance counselor. I was okay with that because I was in a lot of pain, fed up with the abusive home situation, and wanted to get away from the constant fear of living with Stefan and Shelly.

After the nurse popped my hip into place and patched me up a bit, I proceeded to the office of the school guidance counselor. The counselor had me sit down and explain the details of what happened that morning. She sat listening, and she wrote up a report. However, she did not take my story seriously, though I had the wounds, and the testimony of the nurse, on my side. It was as if she just stuck the report (my first report) in her filing cabinet and shrugged the whole thing off!

Despite the guidance counselor's lack of concern, that specific day was a very significant day in my life! On that day, in a school where I had always been the class tease, the class dweeb, the class nerd, and the kid everyone picked on, something drastically different happened. In this school where the kids always made fun of me and picked on me, because I smelled like urine and excretion, looked funny, and acted obnoxious for attention . . . on that day, when they saw my bloody and torn shirt, and my hip out of place, those same kids really cared about me and hugged me! Truth be told, they never saw any physical injury from all their teasing, ostracizing, and picking on me because those were unseen, emotional injuries, though they really did hurt. However, on this day, once my classmates saw my physical and visible injuries, they were moved in compassion to hug me and care about me. Teachers, who did not want to, or know how to, get involved with my situation, suddenly expressed care to me, when they saw the blood and the physical pain, and they also hugged me.

Due to the guidance counselor not taking my case seriously, I was forced to return to the abusive home situation that afternoon. That night, as I laid on the very same cot I had been thrown upon, side and hip hurting me a lot, I reflected on the events of the day. I realized that my being hurt had caused people to express genuine concern for me. Though I had received salvation from God and knew of His love, I still longed for humans to also care about me. God has made me a thinker, so that night I lay there thinking about what the biggest hurt in my life could be. It seemed to me that the best way to see if anyone on earth could really care for me would be to suffer the greatest hurt possible.

As I laid there upon the cot, I concluded that the biggest hurt possible would have to be a vehicle accident and death. So that night I prayed my very first prayer request to God, since my salvation prayer. It was a very specific three-part prayer, because I longed to know someone could really care about me. I asked God to let me get into a vehicle accident. I then asked God to let me die. The third and final part of my prayer was for God to let me hover above my casket, to see if anyone would actually show up and truly care.

Now, for clarity's sake, I have never been suicidal. Even in the midst of all the hell and pain in which I lived, God had placed in me the ability to enjoy and appreciate life in all its beauty. The purpose of my first prayer request was just to know that some human being could really care about me. I really wanted to know for certain that someone could really love me. God, however, in His infinite wisdom and grace, did not grant my prayer request at that time. Instead, I continued on in the abusive home situation.

Chapter 5

Rough Survival and God's Revelations

Shortly after I had accepted Jesus Christ as my Savior, God began to pour out unmerited favor, discernment, and wisdom upon me. I do not consider myself wise in my own eyes, but God had granted me some pretty incredible understanding and wisdom. This enabled me to understand one of the main reasons why Shelly, Stefan, and others were abusing and mistreating me. God revealed to me that it was because of generational curses; a horrible cycle of abuse that had been passed on from generation to generation in their families. It was because they had also been beaten, by people who had been beaten, by people who had been beaten, by people who had been beaten. It was a cycle being passed on from generation to generation.

On one of our visits to Stefan's father's farm, I remember being on the roof of the garage, trying to avoid Shelly and her relentless abuse. Of course, it was a no-no to be on the roof of the garage, but it was always a fun and daring adventure, and a great place to be in hiding. Stefan and Shelly were inside the house visiting with Stefan's parents, when suddenly, the screen door to the farmhouse sprang open like it had been hit by a hurricane. I ducked down, startled, not wanting to be caught up on the roof, but also, with great curiosity, I situated myself so I could see what was happening. Watching what was about to unfold truly impacted my understanding of generational curses.

Perched on top of the garage, I watched Stefan come flying out through the door with his father hobbling rapidly behind him, chasing him; practically tearing Stefan's shirt off and ruthlessly beating him with his cane. I saw blood coming down Stefan's side, as I watched his father chasing him around the yard like a wild animal in a fit of rage. In that moment God really softened my heart toward Stefan and filled me with compassion. God has really protected me from being a vengeful or spiteful person. My heart hurt for Stefan in that moment. I wanted to intervene and help, though I knew I really could not. Witnessing this horrific ordeal allowed me to understand why Stefan was the way he was, and this knowledge was integral in the process of forgiveness that took place well into my teen years, and then in the lifelong process of breaking generational curses and cycles!

I want to be very clear here . . . I do not believe this revelation was given to me as a means to excuse Shelly nor Stefan, as if they had no fault or responsibility for the abuse that they had perpetuated upon Anne, Kate, and me. However, not only did this experience empower me to eventually forgive Stefan and Shelly, it also caused me to make a commitment, right then and there, to break this horrific cycle of rage and senseless abuse. It was there in that moment, at a very young age, that I made a promise to God, to my future wife, to my future children, and to myself; that this abusive, out of control, depraved cycle would never be repeated in me and my future family! It is finished, completed, done, and by the power of God, I walk in victory to this very day!

Another thing I recall happening in the same time-period was that God spoke a very strong word to my heart. He, by His Spirit, convinced me that the name I had been given at birth was a curse placed upon my life, and was not the name that He has written upon His hand and in the eternal Book of Life for me. I had not read the Bible yet, at this point in time, so I didn't know that what God was telling me was also already written in His Word (Isaiah

49:16, Revelation 21:27 NIV)! At that very young age, God gave me an assurance that one day in the future He would reveal my new name to me, and help me through the process of changing it.

Somewhere between the age of seven and nine, I found myself exploring a nearby vacant trailer in the woods, with Kate along with me. In a closet, high up on a shelf over a clothing-rack, there sat a pile of pornographic magazines. By this time, I already knew more about sex and the female anatomy than most people do by the time they are twenty years old. This was partially because Shelly and Stefan seemed to be capable of only two dynamics when it came to their interactions with each other. They were either beating each other or having sex. Anne, Kate, and I were very aware of both aspects, as they were not modest or private about either! Not to mention, a small trailer does not afford a lot of privacy. My knowledge was not just from Shelly and Stefan though, as there were also tremendous amounts of sexual abuse that had taken place to and against me by many different individuals; male and female. Unfortunately, I was no stranger to the female nor the male anatomy, nor to sexual activity.

Even at a very young age, I recognized that physical pleasure came from sexual activity, unfortunately even when it was forced and abusive. While it could cause great trauma, shame, and guilt, the sexual act from an unwanted and unsolicited experience still could cause pleasure. It was confusing and I was repulsed by the forced aspect, but I really was enticed by the female anatomy. Due to my own awakened and over-stimulated sexual mind, I grabbed the pile of pornographic magazines, told Kate not to say anything, and hid them away in my room. They felt like a treasure because it was something I could control and have pleasure over without anyone forcing me. However, before I had ever enjoyed them, Stefan found the pile of magazines. He chose to take away the magazines, and then he would sit with me behind the shed as we looked at the magazines and drank beer together. For years after that, I was exposed to consistent use of alcohol, cigars, and pornography; not only from magazines but also in movies . . . and not only by Stefan, but by other blood and step relatives, and others as well.

I previously had mentioned that being forced to go to bed early and not being allowed to go to the bathroom during the night had resulted in my inability to gain control over my bladder and bowels. As a result, I would occasionally wet myself or even have a bowel movement in my pants right in class. It was incredibly embarrassing, and something I could not explain to my classmates. To make matters worse, Shelly did not wash our clothes very often, and I was seldom allowed to bathe or shower. As a result, I not only smelled awful, but also went around in soiled clothing. All of this caused me to be the target of some persistent bullying, as many classmates continued to pick on me and make fun of me.

One of the most painful and traumatic memories that I have as a child also contributed to even more harassment from my classmates. I was approximately nine years old when Shelly came to my class to speak with a teacher one day. Shelly liked to put on a big show and to be the center of attention. She liked to control and manipulate each situation for her benefit, to make herself look good and get whatever she wanted. On that particular day, Shelly showed up in a rich, shiny, silky dark blue prom dress. For a fleeting moment I was proud of the way she looked, forgetting her very nature. Then she began speaking with the teacher, loud enough for all of the children to hear. The teacher complimented her beautiful dress, and then proceeded to ask why I did not come to school in nice clothes like she was wearing. Her response jolted me horrifically because she said, loud enough for the whole class to hear, "Oh, I don't know. He just doesn't want to. I have tried to get him to, but he just doesn't want to."

Defenseless. Completely defenseless. This adult, who is supposed to be a caring, loving mother figure to me, instead has been punishing me for being born my whole life long. Now, in front of the entire class, she outright lied and said that I am choosing to be filthy, smelly, and crappy. I had no defense because none of the kids or teacher would believe me over the adult. I hated being filthy and without control of my bodily functions. I hated not being able to wash and be clean. I hated that I had limited, feces infested, urine drenched clothing, which Shelly seldom washed. I was crushed. There are not adequate words to express the pain of this injustice and false accusation. I had now encountered yet another level of the extent of abuse Shelly could and would dish out, so she could make herself look good.

As I continued on in the abusive home situation, I adopted two main approaches for continuing forward. The first approach was to stay as far away from Shelly and Stefan as I could. Living on a property in the woods, I would escape into the woods as often as possible. I also would try not to say much of anything, if I had to be around Shelly, so as not to upset her. When it was not possible to be away from Stefan, I would work hard and try to be on his good side, hoping to experience some compassion from him.

I remember one day when Stefan was probably the most enraged that I had ever seen him. I do not recall why he was so enraged, but I do remember that I immediately jumped out the nearest window and ran for the woods. He came charging after me, but I had gotten enough of a head start to be able to climb a massive V-shaped pine tree that branched off with two big trunks, that sat right on the edge of the forest behind the trailer. Being as small as I was, I was able to quickly climb high up into the tree, close to the top. Stefan arrived at the bottom and kept screaming all sorts of profanity at me. I remember him swearing that he was going to kill me, and my body's response was strange to me. I laughed and cried at the same time from a mixed sense of great fear and great victory, as my body quivered from both sensations. Then Stefan left briefly, only to return with his chain saw. I knew, from all my work logging and cutting down trees with him, that the base of this tree was too big for him to actually cut all the way through with his small chainsaw, so I just waited for him to calm down. I also was well aware that he was truly in a rage and really wanted to kill me, but I felt proud of myself for having gotten away. I'd hate to think what might have happened if he had caught me!

After several minutes of Stefan's cutting at the base of the tree, which felt more like hours to me, Shelly came out and yelled at him to just leave me alone. He screamed out to me that it wasn't over yet, but then put the chainsaw back in the shed. I stayed in the tree for quite a while, and when I came down, he had cooled off so much that he just smacked me upside the head and laughed. I really felt

God's hand had been on me in that situation, as He protected me and changed Stefan's heart, at least momentarily.

The second approach that I adopted was focused on a mentality of gaining victory over Shelly. I was determined to find ways to 'win' against her manipulation, by outwitting her. As a woman who craved power and control, and longed to constantly punish me, she would often not know how to respond, even if only for just a split second, when I went above and beyond whatever she expected, or I acted nice though she was being intentionally mean. Sometimes gaining victory and winning against her meant I had to take pleasure in things she had designed to remove pleasure. Other times I 'won' by taking pleasure in the things she couldn't control. Another way I 'won' and received pleasure was by breaking into the dry freezer. Here I found a great value in raw oatmeal, brown sugar, and especially raw spaghetti and pasta! It was a matter of survival and victory, to know how to 'win' in different situations because, the Lord knows, I surely lost in a majority of the situations in my childhood.

Chapter 6

Used

An amazing aspect of jars is that they each get used independently of their own circumstances or decisions. The potter or owner has a purpose for them. Throughout my childhood, living in the abusive situation, there was an aspect of my life for which only God gets all the glory. When I accepted Jesus Christ as my Savior, I accepted His eternal gift of salvation. However, I was unaware that He desires a daily, love relationship with me. God was faithful though, even in my earliest years, to use me and my life to reveal Himself, even and especially without me knowing or realizing that He was at work in me! The Potter was already using me as a JAR for His glory!

While I was living in immense abuse, being used as a punching bag verbally, physically, sexually, mentally, and emotionally, God was using my life differently. In my Sunday school class, Shannon provided all sorts of competitions encouraging us to regularly attend Sunday School, read our Bibles, memorize scripture, and to bring friends with us as well. Her prizes were always exciting and worth the extra effort: pizza parties, ice cream-sundae parties, a trip to her parents' beach-front lake house, roller-skating, bowling, etc. Fortunately, God blessed me with a great memory and academic ability, so I always memorized the scriptures and was always one of the firsts, if not the first, to win the competitions and prizes. I enjoyed the learning, the competition, and being good at something. These competitions offered me lots of pleasures and opportunities that were not afforded to me in the abusive home!

During the time while I was between seven and ten years old, Shannon also came to my school on a weekly basis to provide a Good News Club after school. This is a ministry of Child Evangelism Fellowship—also known as CEF. I remember the day when she announced that CEF was hosting a competition throughout the six New England states to see which child could create the best Christmas card. The winner would receive a free week at the CEF *Camp Good News*. My heart longed to have the opportunity to go to camp, though it seemed like such an unlikely chance with my life circumstances; coming from a home of poverty and abuse, and with Shelly always trying to remove pleasure. Though it also seemed to be a far-fetched fairytale, especially since the competition expanded across six different states, there was still a hint of hope and excitement that bubbled up in me! I was excited to try to win this competition!

As Shannon handed out the supplies, she encouraged all of us to enter the competition. I participated also because I thought it was a neat experience to join in a competition that stretched throughout all of New England! Although I was still unaware of the constant daily love relationship God longed for with me, I did know without a doubt what the best Christmas present was. It was obviously baby Jesus, so I drew, or perhaps I should say that I feebly attempted to draw, a manger with baby Jesus in it. I wrote something like, "God's greatest gift at Christmas" and then gave the card to Shannon to submit. The competition then faded away from my attention and focus, and quickly became forgotten.

A few months later, as I was attending Vacation Bible School, Shannon and Mary (another lady from the church) showed up dressed as clowns with a big bunch of balloons. All of us kids were surprised and so excited! We had no clue why clowns were arriving, but it was exciting! Shannon then told us that someone from our church had won the CEF Christmas card competition. As I looked around the room, I had the winner narrowed down to one of two kids. With my lack of artistic ability, it certainly wasn't going to be me. Then Shannon and Mary shouted out together, "And the winner is . . . J.R."

I was dumbfounded! Could this be true? Really? Were they just playing an awful trick on me? In that moment though, I sensed God's hand on me, a great peace came over me, and I sensed God's hand of favor and protection. Somehow God had used little me to create a Christmas card that would be sent out throughout all the six states of New England for CEF! He had granted His favor and blessing for my card design to win, so that I might be blessed with a free week at Camp Good News!

Not only did I win the competition, but I was also invited to a CEF donors' banquet in the largest city in Maine, Portland, to be recognized for my creation of the Christmas card. Shannon drove a group of us children from her Sunday school class to the banquet. I will never forget her long brownish/yellowish station wagon, with a back door with a long window that could be lowered, and the cool red pop-up seats in the very back. She packed her car with kids, including Anne, Kate and me. Shannon had helped get us into nice clean clothes, and to also be relatively clean. I could tell Anne and Kate were a little jealous for the recognition I would be receiving, and I remember wishing there was some way I could share it with them.

We arrived at the convention center and entered into the extravagantly decorated ballroom filled with lots of people, all dressed up and looking very important. I remember feeling excited about this adventure, as Shannon showed us to our table. I was not nervous at all! Shannon definitely had her hands full though, with a bunch of excited children. She had lots of patience with us though, and was able to handle us lovingly and effectively.

As a little boy, who was being intentionally deprived of food, I now found myself sitting before a gorgeously set table with a marvelous feast that felt like it had been prepared for kings! I was so thankful to God for the food, as well as for all the happy people all around! It was an exciting moment that I will never forget. It didn't matter that I lived in poverty and was unloved, I was still invited into this banquet!

After the dinner, Child Evangelism Fellowship leaders recognized me for the Christmas card, and all these really important looking people all around me stood and applauded me. It was an unforgettable moment. Was I only dreaming? Were they really applauding *me*? In that moment, God impressed upon me that He wanted to use my life to reveal Himself to others so they would come to know the truth of His love for His creation. He also made it very clear in my heart and mind that my life had been created to be used for His glory. It was a fingerprint of God on my life, telling me that He has called me. Even as a young boy, not yet surrendered to God's absolute authority and lordship in my life, I knew that I was firmly in the hands of the Potter.

Though I did not fully understand what it meant at that moment, I treasured in my heart the awesome blessing of winning the competition, being able to be at the banquet, and then being able to go to summer camp for a week for free. For some reason, God chose to make Himself evident through the life of a very weak, poor, wretched little boy . . . the youngest of a poor, depraved, and broken family. God, the Potter, was already using me as a vessel, a mere little boy, to share His truth, love, and goodness with others. He also was lavishing me with His great love and favor.

Chapter 7

Run Boy, Run!

When I was ten years old, I finally got so fed up with the abuse that I decided to run away. I waited until a very rainy night, when Shelly and Stefan were both away at work. Anne, Kate, and I had been left home alone to fend for ourselves often, and this was just another night like the others, but I had made up my mind. As I prepared to leave, Anne and Kate begged and pleaded with me not to go, but I could not be deterred. They continued begging me and crying and cursing as I ran out into the pouring rain.

I was planning on fleeing the state; either traveling to the warmth and beaches of Florida, or leaving the country and venturing off into Canada. Maine is situated on the border of Canada, near Quebec, so in my mind that would be an easy escape option. My plan that night was to run a few miles down the road to a classmate's house, to see if I could stay there for the night, and then to go into the city the next day to find a way out of the state. I would choose my final destination the next day.

As I was fleeing the abusive home, it was dark out and sheets of rain were coming down all around me. Traveling along the edge of the country road, I would duck down into gutters or quickly sneak into the woods when I saw headlights approaching. I knew the rain would give me an advantage of seeing oncoming cars before the drivers would be able to see me. After walking several miles, I arrived at the home of one of my classmates, and I was quickly welcomed in. Her parents were very nice to me, and they gave me some cookies, a drink, and an umbrella. However, they then decided they should notify the police. While they were making the phone call, I knew I had to get away, so I just ran out the door. I visited the home of three or four other classmates that night, and every time the same thing would occur. The parents would welcome me in, be very nice, give me snacks, rain gear, and warm clothes, but then would contact the authorities. I finally decided to give up on classmates and made the plan that I would hike back to Shannon and Willy's big farm, though it was so close to where Shelly and Stefan lived.

Shannon and Willy own a large berry farm business, and they had a large barn with lots of bales of straw to cover over the strawberries for the winter, (hence the name straw-berries). I thought I could just sneak into their barn, sleep in the straw for the night until very early morning, and then leave the state the next day. As I approached their farm though, the dog was outside and, even in the rain, he could smell my stench and started barking. I quickly ducked into the woods on the other side of the road, hid behind a large tree, and I became very still. Almost immediately Willy came outside, called the dog, and then started yelling my name, "J.R." very loudly. I just remained very still, not only because I did not want to be found, but also because I was frozen in fear. Anne and Kate had obviously informed Willy and Shannon that I had run away.

These new circumstances caused for me to have to immediately change my plans once again. Good thing God had made me quick on my feet. I determined that I would just wait for Willy to go back inside, and then I would head off on foot for approximately twelve to fifteen miles to get to the city. I would sleep under a big bridge over the Androscoggin River that connects Auburn and Lewiston, and then I could flee the state the next morning. Canada was very close, but Florida was always a dream location for me, as I have always loved beaches, heat, and sun! So, once Willy went inside and took the dog in with him, I headed off for the city!

That night the rain was coming down in torrents. I had only continued to run less than two miles from Shannon and Willy's farm, and, as I approached a sharp corner in the road, I did not see the headlights of an oncoming car quick enough to get out of sight. Unfortunately, it was a patrol car, and the police were looking for me. I immediately just laid down in the gutter, frozen in fear, hoping and praying they had not seen me, but the car came to a screeching halt right next to me. An officer abruptly got out of the car, picked me up, and put me into the back seat. He verified my name and told me I was in a lot of trouble for making a lot of people worried. I had a strong sense of defeat as he took me back to the trailer. I also doubted that many people, if any, were truly all that worried about me. My heart sank that I would not be making it to the beautiful sunny beaches of Florida, as that was where my decision had landed, as I had been running in the cold rain.

Evidently, Anne and Kate had contacted lots of people when I had left, including Shelly and Stefan. Both of them left work early to return to the trailer, and neither was happy. The police officers took me to the door and Shelly invited them in. She convinced them that everything was fine; that I was just acting out. She also convinced the officers that I thought it would be funny to run away and cause a scene. She then asked one policeman to threaten me. I remember the tall figure of the officer as he was towering over me, with a gun at his side, sternly threatening to throw me in jail if I ever ran away again.

It is rather ironic, because I distinctly remember my exact thought as the officer leaned down in my face and threatened that the next time he would throw me in jail. I thought, '*It has got to be better than this!*' Jail would be a relief in comparison to the abusive home situation. It just had to be better than the situation I was living in! I didn't say anything though, except to promise the officer I would behave, because I was fearful of upsetting anyone, or getting into even more trouble.

After the policeman left, I got one of the worst beatings of my life from both Shelly and Stefan. They had no concern for me, but they were furious about having to leave work and that I had caused a big, community-wide stir involving the police. I had embarrassed them by my actions. I am certain that I had the presence of protective and faithful angels that night, as I am sure my survival through their beatings was truly supernatural.

Chapter 8

Locked Up

When I was ten or eleven years old, Shelly, in her deceit and manipulation, convinced the State of Maine's Department of Human Services (DHS) that Kate and I both needed to be placed into separate mental institutes. Shelly used my running away, nightly head-banging, and the pornography and inappropriate sexual behavior as support for my need of treatment. She also made up some pretty exaggerated lies about both Kate and me.

The irony is that Anne, who was the only one remaining in the abusive home situation at this time, was the one who had actually received some brain damage from the abusive treatment that she had suffered as a baby. She really lacked in mental processing and common sense. Shelly's mental state was also another case of irony. She also obviously had mental deficits from the abuse she suffered as a child. I'm not saying this out of hate or spite, but rather as an honest observation and deduction from the reality of her past. Nonetheless, she was able to convince the State of Maine to place Kate and me into two separate mental institutions, in two different cities.

On the night that I arrived at the psychiatric ward, I was placed in a room with a fourteen-year-old boy who was almost seven-feet tall; resulting from an uncontrollable growth hormone disorder. His body was growing considerably faster than his mind, and he was just not able to handle the abnormal growth in a sane manner. That night he forced himself on me sexually, and due to his size and strength I was unable to defend myself nor resist. I quickly reported the situation to the staff early the next morning, and they then placed me into my own room with my own bathroom. I don't ever remember seeing the fourteen-year-old boy again.

During my first week in the mental institution, I really battled with some deep questions. I have always been a deep thinker and my mind is always working. In that psychiatric ward, I began to think about, and ask myself, "Am I really mental? Did I make up the whole experience when I was seven and accepted Jesus Christ? Am I abnormal, insane, and/or out of my mind?" I struggled with these thoughts for about a week. God was faithful to provide another blessing and fingerprint in my life, to answer those questions.

There was a young lady, in her twenties, if my memory serves me correctly, whom I will call Julie. Julie did some modeling in New York, but was originally from Maine. She was also studying in the medical/psychological field, and she volunteered her time at the mental facility I was in. At night, it was her job to close down the psychiatric ward. First, she would go to the padded rooms and to the people in straitjackets. Then, she would check on the rooms with dual occupancy. Julie would then make her way to the hall of single rooms. Each night that she worked, her last stop of the night would be my room. She would bring a plate or tray of goodies and drinks, and just sit down and talk with me. She treated me like a normal human being. She helped me to feel normal and special.

One night, towards the end of my first week there, I felt like I had almost driven myself crazy with the anguish of finding the answer to my questions about my own sanity. Julie came into my room that night with goodies and drinks. She set them down on my desk and sat down at the end of my bed. It was obvious that she had been crying and was upset. She told me to come sit next to her. She wrapped her arm around my shoulders, ran her fingers through my hair like a mother would, and said, "I need you to know that you are not the reason why you have been placed here. There are people outside these walls who belong here instead of you. The doctors can find nothing wrong with you, but they are going to classify you as depressed and keep you here for a month." She continued on to tell me the state of Maine was paying a large sum of money daily for me to be there, because Shelly couldn't afford it. In other words, the hospital was benefiting from me being there, so they did not want to release me! God used Julie, right then and there, to answer my questions and concerns, and to convince me that I was not insane!

A little side note that I want to place here . . . somehow God the Potter has never allowed depression to truly be a part of my journey. Praise His holy name! I have been sad, frustrated, angry, deceived, confused, etc. but really have never had to battle depression. I know several friends who do battle depression, and I do not make light of the true battle that it is for them. It was very ironic that the doctors chose that diagnosis for me though, as most people who know me can testify that I am usually full of energy, excitement, and vibrant life. I love life, each and every day!

My next comment may seem like the most mental thing anyone could ever say about being incorrectly placed into a mental institute, but if you read on, you will understand. That month in the psychiatric ward was the biggest vacation, and some of the most pleasurable times, of my first thirteen years of life! I had my own clean bed, a soft mattress, my own clean sheets, my own pillow, my own clean blankets, and even my own bathroom and shower! Everything was new and very clean. I had a door that I could close, and somehow feel a little more protected. I could sleep well, without fear of a beating! I could go to the bathroom whenever I needed! I could shower whenever I wanted! I could wear clean clothes all the time! I could have three meals a day AND I was able to choose whatever I wanted to eat! I could have sugared cereals, eggs, bacon, waffles, pancakes, pasta, meat, seafood, etc. I could even have snacks! It was definitely one of my favorite periods of time in my first thirteen years of life!

The majority of the staff, knowing of my specific circumstances, treated me like a king while I was there. They said I was the model patient, and they gave me special privileges, like going outside to throw a frisbee and kick a ball around. They were all aware of the fact that I was not mentally disturbed, nor depressed. It's amazing to me how God uses even the greed of man for His glory and purposes. I believe God wanted me to have relief and freedom from the abuse, and thus allowed the doctors to want the income from the state so much that they would diagnose me as depressed. I thank God for the wonderful time I had there. It was an amazing fingerprint of a generous and loving Potter, Father God!

It's amazing how many times, and the various ways, God used what Shelly meant as punishment or an effort to remove pleasure as a means to bring me more freedom and pleasure! For example, Shelly's decision to let Anne, Kate, and me attend church with Shannon and Willy had been an attempt to get us out of the house and out of her sight, while also trying to ensure the removal of pleasure as well. However, it was through her selfish decision that I received the greatest blessing of all by inviting Jesus Christ into my heart and life, as my Savior. Now, being placed in a psychiatric ward, was another one of Shelly's attempts to remove pleasure from my life. However, my time in this institution was amazing! Personally, I think God has a great sense of humor, and He laughed with joy at the pleasure, happiness, and freedom I received while being locked up there.

Julie was right though, and I was kept at the psychiatric ward for just under a month. The doctors declared that I had quickly recovered from my depression, and I was released to return to the abusive home situation. The 'home' environment had improved slightly, even if just physically, because, while I was in the psychiatric ward, Stefan had purchased a new trailer, an artisan well, and the new place had running water and a water heater. Now I also had my own room, and not just a cot in the living room. I did only have the small cot mattress to sleep on, on the floor, but it was more comfortable than the metal spring cot.

It became apparent though, that Shelly believed that she had gotten rid of Kate and me for good, because when I returned to the abusive home situation her already intense abuse toward me escalated even more. It was also evident that Kate had acquired some of Shelly's manipulative behaviors, as she was able to use the mental institute as an escape from the abuse and depravity. While I was in the psychiatric ward for less than a month, Kate remained institutionalized for over six months, and she seemed to greatly enjoy it. I do not fault her at all, for being wise in using that place as a refuge from the abuse.

Chapter 9

Pounded Again

There is an instance of physical abuse worth mentioning, that occurred when I was somewhere between the age of eleven and thirteen years old. Although it wasn't the worst abuse Kate, Anne, and I experienced, it paints a clear picture of the intensity of the physical abuse that we often lived with. The sexual, mental, verbal, and emotional abuse are too hard, and in some ways too inappropriate, to share.

It was a Sunday afternoon, and Shannon and Willy were returning Kate, Anne, and me to the abusive living situation. As we arrived, Shelly was outside feeding the dogs. Anne, Kate, and I walked into the trailer, and, as we entered, we encountered Stefan, who was in an uncontrollable rage. He was standing in the kitchen, cursing and complaining about the dirty dishes and the new trailer now being a pigpen. He started screaming at us, "Who is going to do the dishes and do them now?" The quotation is minus a lot of inappropriate and profane language that he had used.

We had entered into the trailer with Kate at the front, and I was following Anne, who was right behind her. As soon as we heard Stefan in his rage, Kate and I quickly and wisely managed to scurry into our bedrooms. Unfortunately, because of the brain damage Anne had received from the abuse when she was a baby, she lacked common sense and had not recognized the negative effect of responding to Stefan when he was in a rage. She turned towards him and said, "Just let me put my Bible in my room, and then I'll wash the dishes." She said it sweetly, and there was no sarcasm nor any way to misinterpret her meaning. She planned to go to her room, put her Bible down, and come back to do the dishes.

One might think that Anne's nice response would resolve Stefan's anger and the tense situation. However, just Anne's talking to Stefan set him off even more, and he came racing down the hall toward her. He grabbed her Bible and started ripping it, and then threw it on the floor. He then began beating Anne. He grabbed her by her ponytail and slammed her head against the wall. At that point, Kate came running out of her bedroom screaming and swearing at Stefan. She smacked and kicked him as she passed by him, and then ran from him into the master bedroom. He was infuriated even more, and chased after her, leaving Anne crumpled on the floor crying.

By this time, Shelly had heard the commotion from outside and came running in the front door, and she followed Stefan into the master bedroom. I ran out of my room and followed Shelly into the master bedroom. I entered the room in time to see Stefan holding Kate down on the bed; pounding his fist into her head and body. His face was red and his eyes showed that he had lost control.

Shelly tried getting between Stefan and Kate, but then Stefan just pushed Shelly onto the bed and started beating her. At this point, I jumped on the bed, tried pushing Stefan off Shelly, and screamed at him to stop before he killed someone. I truly believe that, on numerous occasions if God had not intervened, he truly would have killed one of us, while he was out of control and enraged.

In an effort to distract Stefan, while I yelled at him, I also kicked at his head. His reaction time was still really good though, and he caught my leg in his hand as it came close to his head. He thrust me off the back side of the bed. I landed on the corner of the bureau and crumpled to the floor. Stefan came running around the bed, screaming that he was going to kill someone and that 'that someone' was going to be me. He then dropped his knee into my side, pinned me to the floor, and began pounding me repeatedly.

Shelly then got up and came running around the bed. She shoved Stefan out the door of the master bedroom, and shut and locked the door. Then things calmed down and returned to normal, or as 'normal' as they could be in the abusive home.

I share these hard situations not for pity, but so you might join me in praising God Almighty, for both His rescue and redemption of my life. Perhaps now you understand why my story often moves me to praise the Potter. His fingerprints and times of protection and intervention in my life have been numerous.

Another traumatic beating occurred when I was thirteen years old, and it really made me determined that I would never allow myself, nor anyone else, to be abused ever again, so long as I could prevent it. It was a Sunday, in the middle of a cold, snowy Maine winter. We had all gone to visit Stefan's family, at his father's farm in Durham, and we were now making the long drive back to the trailer, in the midst of a fierce snow storm. As we entered the city of Auburn, driving right next to the Androscoggin River off to our right, Shelly was in the driver's seat and Stefan was in the front passenger seat. I was sitting in the middle in the back seat between Anne and Kate. We were approaching the first traffic light, where a pickup truck had just stopped in front of us. Though we were not traveling very fast, Shelly tried to stop, but the car slid on the snowy road right into the back of the pickup truck in front of us.

Though it was an accident, and we were all surprised by it, Stefan became immediately enraged. He reached across the car and punched Shelly in the face. I became defensive for her, because I knew she had not intentionally hit the truck. Though Shelly abused me and deprived me so very often, in this moment she was just as shocked and upset as the rest of us, and God had given me a compassionate heart. When Stefan hit her, I laid out a whole line of curse words at him. In my righteous indignation, I did not consider what the consequences would be for defending Shelly.

God has created in me a sense of righteous indignation against injustice, but at this young age I had not yet partnered it with wisdom from God regarding how and when to use it. Stefan grew even more enraged at my attempt to defend Shelly, so he turned around and punched me in the face. He then wrapped his hands and fingers

JAR: A Vessel in the Hands of the Potter

around my neck and started choking me; swearing that he was going to kill me! I'm confident, if it weren't for God's supernatural intervention, that he really would have killed me right then and there. However, all praise to God, another fingerprint of the Potter instantly occurred in that moment.

I believe that it was a fingerprint of God that the accident took place right next to a donut shop and bakery. There was a police officer sitting in his car in the parking lot, right next to the donut shop. However, due to the amount of snow that was falling all around the car, the officer could not see what Stefan was doing to me. He definitely had witnessed the accident though, and quickly approached the car. As he began knocking on Stefan's window, Shelly shouted at Stefan to let him know that a police officer was standing at the window. For the first time in my life, I saw fear in Stefan's eyes. He instantly snapped out of his rage, released his death grip on my neck, and sat back into his seat quickly. Air gushed into my lungs and I sat back in my seat, relieved that Stefan had let me go, and even more relieved that there was an officer at the window, though my fear of Stefan kept me from actually saying anything. I sat there, crying in pain, fear, and frustration.

In that moment something even more dramatic happened to me. For in the moment, as the officer stood at the window, I finally knew beyond a shadow of a doubt that it was over. Never again would I allow myself to be in an abusive situation, so far as I could prevent it. Shelly and Stefan's screaming at each other was a common occurrence. Their exchange of angry words often escalated to physical fighting. This explanation is not to excuse their violence, but usually it was provoked between the two. However, this time Shelly had done nothing wrong, and there had been no provocation for Stefan to hit her. It was at that moment that I made a commitment that I would never allow myself to be in or remain in an abusive situation, and I knew that I would also fight for others to not have to experience abuse either. I give all glory and praise to God for His fingerprint because this was a pivotal moment that brought about some great change!

Chapter 10

Reported Again

The day after the car accident I returned to school. I was in sixth grade. I vividly remember that my classroom was right across the hall from the nurse's office, the guidance counselor's office, and the bathrooms. It took a while, but I finally got up the courage to ask my teacher for permission to go to the guidance counselor's office. I knew I had to share my story with an adult, and hoped that somehow, he or she could and would work to help me get rescued.

The first time I had reported any abuse was after Stefan had beaten me bloody when I was seven years old; leaving me barely able to walk. Three years after that incident, the first guidance counselor was let go. I heard that it was because of negligence. Evidently, there were several cases, mine included, where she was negligent in completing and submitting important forms. However, there was a statute of limitations preventing all our cases from being reopened or assessed. However, on this particular Monday morning, after the car accident where Stefan tried to strangle me, I walked into the new guidance counselor's office and reported to her the abuse that Kate, Anne and I were experiencing. She took me seriously. In fact, she called Anne and Kate from their classes to her office, and they verified that I was telling the truth.

Once I had made the report of abuse, and Anne and Kate had confirmed it, the guidance counselor then called the State of Maine Department of Human Services (DHS) and the State of Maine Police. Soon after that there were two social workers from the DHS and two state police officers in the guidance counselor's office with us. After they all met behind closed doors for a while, one of the policemen kindly explained that we needed to return to the trailer to retrieve our belongings, and he invited me to ride with him in his police car. Anne and Kate went with the social workers in their car. I not sure how much we realized or knew that we were taking our last trip ever back to the trailer where we had suffered so much abuse. However, I do recall that I had a great hope in my heart that life somehow was about to change for the better!

I have always had a childlike and playful spirit, and I remember how excited I was to be in a police car on good terms (unlike the situation when I ran away). The police officers were very nice. One even used his radar gun on oncoming cars, and he told me to turn on the siren and lights to warn the oncoming traffic that they were going too fast. I really enjoyed it!

Many thoughts were racing through my head as we rode toward the trailer in the police car, though. Maybe Shelly and Stefan would be threatened by the police officers about jail, or maybe they would actually be arrested and the three of us kids could live together in the trailer by ourselves. Maybe I would never again fear for my life, hang on to the edge of life after an intense physical beating, never again be forced to have sex or do inappropriate sexual things, never be told how dirty, stupid, ugly, and unwanted I was, nor feel threatened or be abused again. Maybe Stefan would fight the police and lose. Maybe the police would really see the abusive home for the true reality it had been for us. Maybe, just maybe, we would finally truly be rescued, and offered a new home and life that could be full and beautiful! Maybe the police would be like the firefighter in the decal from the bedroom on Vine St. Maybe they would truly care and rescue us!

Chapter 11

Rescued

As we arrived at the trailer, the police officers told us to stay with the social workers until they would advise us when it was safe to enter. It was obvious that the police were taking our report seriously, and they wanted to check out the situation with Shelly and Stefan before allowing us into the trailer. As we waited, the social workers gave each of us a big thick black garbage bag, and then advised us to grab whatever we wanted from our rooms that could fit in the bags, and then to quickly come back out. After a few minutes, one of the police officers came to the front door and motioned that it was safe for us to come in. With our garbage bags in hand, we entered the trailer.

What I saw as I entered the trailer for my very last time was a pretty traumatic experience. However, it was an experience that brought some finality to the life situation in which I, Anne, and Kate had been living for so long! Stefan was seated at the dining room table with his back to me. Obviously, he had put up a fight, because one of the policemen was restraining him with his pistol drawn. The other officer was standing between the dining room table and the master bedroom door telling Shelly not to come out of her room or he would shoot. He announced that we were entering just to get some of our belongings, and that Stefan and Shelly needed to remain calm and wait for us to leave.

Anne, Kate, and I went to our rooms quickly. I will never forget walking in my room for the last time. It was completely empty, save a thin mattress on the floor near the wall, with a blanket on it that was saturated in urine and excretion. The walls were also empty because I was never allowed to hang anything on them, but then I never owned anything to put on them anyway. I took one final look around the empty 'prison' and walked out with an empty garbage bag. I was fine having nothing to bring with me from the abusive home, because I wanted to leave that place, those people, and all that pain far, far behind. I was ready to start a new chapter, new season, and a new way of life.

When I reported the abuse, the counselor had obviously alerted the social workers that Stefan had often threatened to kill us if we ever told anyone. As a result, the DHS placed us into protective custody; moving us around the state of Maine in different locations so that Stefan would not be able to find us. There were a few quick stays in homes of people who attended church with Shannon and Willy, and/or lived relatively nearby. Then we were placed with a very nice family way up in northern Maine, near the Canadian border, where we remained for several months. The DHS was working hard to keep the three of us together, while also preventing Stefan and Shelly from being able to find us.

Another fingerprint of the Potter in my life appeared during the first few months of being in the state's custody. At some point in those first few months, I was lying on a bed and had my Bible next to me. I randomly opened it, and found myself looking at the book of James, chapter 3, which was titled, "Taming the Tongue." At that time, I had a very colorful and profane vocabulary, which I used often. Somehow, in a very supernatural way, as I was reading the wise words of James, God chose to free me from the profanity. He not only took the profanity off my tongue, but rightly convicted me of the importance of guarding my words, and using them to be life-giving! It was a supernatural fingerprint of the Potter, because the vulgar words I had spoken for thirteen years were instantly gone in a split second! Although I could not tame my tongue, God certainly could and did!

After those first several months in foster care, the DHS decided that Anne, Kate, and I would be placed in Shannon and Willy's home. Shannon and Willy had agreed to take us in because they wanted to help keep us together. This excited me because I could not have asked for a better home environment. However, the location also gave me great fear, as we were less than a mile down the road from Shelly and Stefan. Many nights I remember running to the bathroom, closing and locking the door, after waking up from flash backs of different episodes of abuse. I would curl up on the floor in a fetal position, sweating and crying out of fear. Shannon and Willy could not understand my fear or actions. Praise God for His eventual victory over this fear in my life, as He healed me in so many ways, with His beautiful fingerprints all over me.

Since I was in the womb, I've always desired to belong in a family where I was loved and wanted. Moving in with Shannon and Willy elevated my hopes that I could now become part of such a family! I was elated and hopeful! Shortly after moving in with them, I recall asking Shannon and Willy if Kate, Anne, and I could start calling them 'mom' and 'dad'. They are wonderful people, with beautiful, loving hearts, but they really had their hands tied because of the legal system of foster care, and with their own different expectations than mine. Though I could not understand their reasoning at the time, they told us that we would not be able to call them 'mom' and 'dad'. Their preference was that we should call them by their first names, because we were only going to stay with them temporarily, until the DHS could find us a successful placement, to keep the three of us together. Since I was still young and hopeful for a family, this crushed me and my hopes of being a part of their family. From that time forward, I protected myself by never allowing myself to think nor believe they wanted me as part of their family. Whatever the reason and purpose, I sensed a feeling of rejection and knew that, though I was in their home, I was an outsider in their family. They were a great and godly family, I just was not truly a part of it.

Shannon and Willy were an amazing source of blessing, encouragement, and strength for me in the time I lived with their family. I know that at some point Shannon, Willy, and their children may read these words. My hope is they will each know the very special place they have in my heart, and just how much love and appreciation I have for them. I understand that what they did was a godly, loving act of trying to help us remain together. Their reasons were valid, though they differed from what my hopes had been. May they be greatly blessed for all their sacrifices and investments in me and my life!

Chapter 12

Who Will Love Me?

Having just been rescued, placed into the foster care system, and yet not really finding a family to belong to or to be a part of, I decided I would strive to pursue receiving attention, recognition, and acceptance elsewhere. Being in the custody of the state's Department of Human Services, life was drastically different. I was now allowed to bathe daily. I was no longer sleeping in a soiled and disgusting bed, going to the bathroom out of fear, but rather I was allowed and encouraged to use the toilet. Learning to control my bladder and bowels was difficult and humiliating. However, the fact that I never again had to wear clothing soiled with urine and excrement, nor be dirty without bathing, was a huge blessing. I love to bathe and to take nice hot showers!

When we were taken into the state's custody, Anne, Kate, and I each received a large voucher of money from the DHS to go shopping for new clothes. So, although I had returned to the same school where I was always made fun of and teased for how I smelled, looked, and acted, I was now clean, fashionable, and free to participate in all the activities, events, and programs that I wanted to at school. I was also allowed to have friends and have some sense of normality in life. I could eat whatever I wanted, dress fashionably, have friends, and truly enjoy the gift of life God had given me!

In the new situation I found myself living, I was now also allowed to participate in extra-curricular activities. I was excited to try sports. Someone gave me a basketball and shooting seemed to come naturally to me. I could knock in some 3-point shots, at least until someone was playing against me. If someone wanted to play knock-out, h.o.r.s.e, or another shooting game I could definitely compete, but when it was an actual game I was sure to be one of the last ones picked. For some reason, having a defender playing against me made me 'butterfingers' and I couldn't control the ball, nor play very well.

One day though, someone gave me a soccer ball. I felt like it just clicked for me. I could have several defenders against me and yet I was determined to get the ball in the goal! I started playing pretty well and I fell in love with soccer! In fact, I loved it so much, at that time, that it became like a god to me. I worshipped it, idolized it, and served it with all I was. I became good enough that I was certain that I would be playing varsity in my freshman year of high school. I aspired to be a professional soccer player. Soccer became a priority and god to me.

Another new avenue for receiving attention, at this time, was in my academic performance. To this point, I had always done well academically. In fact, in my younger years, while in the abusive home situation, the teachers had wanted to move me to a higher grade for my academic abilities. However, while I was living in the abusive home Shelly never was willing for that to happen, probably because she did not want me to receive favor and pleasure from it. One thing she could not control or take from me in those years though, was my ability and desire to excel academically. Up until this point, my academic ability was just one more thing that the kids had held against me, thinking that I was a nerd. Now that I was clean, fashionable, athletic, and a smart kid I really was enjoying lots of attention, popularity, and recognition. As a result, academics and popularity also became like gods to me. In reality, much of what motivated me was that I just wanted to feel loved and accepted, and being recognized and appreciated for my different strengths was what was available to me for the time being.

Another advantage of being clean, wearing nice clothes, excelling academically, and participating in athletics was the attention I was getting from girls. Girls at school and in my church youth group started talking to me and flirting with me. I enjoyed the flirtation, but due to the serious sexual abuse in my first thirteen years of life, I could flirt back, but wouldn't act upon it. It scared me. Though I wanted a romantic relationship, I had experienced sex in so many violating ways I needed tremendous healing. I also really needed God to show me healthy and accurate placement and use of sex. Though my body had been awakened to sexual stimulation by force and abuse as a mere infant and throughout my childhood, once I had been rescued from the abusive home situation I never again had sex, in the first twenty years of my life. I did, however, allow girls to become a bit of an obsession, sometimes objects of impure thoughts and conversations, and another idol in my life.

Though these four idols . . . soccer, academics, popularity, and girls . . . had popped up in my life, God was faithful to continue patiently and lovingly work in my heart and life. During the summers in foster care, the foster parents were offered respite (time away) from the foster children (another thing that showed me that I really was not completely part of the family of Shannon and Willy) to have time with their own children and family. The Department of Human Services paid for me to go away to a Christian camp. I attended and greatly enjoyed Camp Berea, throughout the summers of my teen years, and, though I did not recognize it at the time, the Potter was already working in me for healing and victory.

My first summer at Camp Berea was an experience in which the late director, Mr. Glen Chaffee, an incredible man and reflection of God, taught me some of the discipline and grace of God. During my first week at camp, we were repeatedly told not to kick the volleyball. Due to some juvenile jealousy and competition for the attention of one of the girls at camp, one day I was so upset that I kicked the volleyball. In my anger I kicked it so hard that the force of the kick popped the volleyball. It definitely was *not* a soccer ball, and was not meant to be kicked!

Mr. Chaffee came up to me later that afternoon, gently wrapped his arm around my shoulder, and asked me to tell him honestly if I had been the one who had kicked the volleyball. As I confessed, he sadly shared with me that I was going to be sent back to the foster home for that week. He continued lovingly to tell me that I was welcome to come back the next week, after I was able to calm down and consider my behavior. He was stern, but oozed with the love of Jesus. He assured me that he would be waiting with arms open for me, that next week.

I did return the next week, and Mr. Chaffee was indeed awaiting my arrival, alongside the staff, and they all embraced me and welcomed me! I then returned for a few more weeks of camp that summer, and even was awarded the Camper of the Week award one of those weeks! I spent all my summers of my teen years at Camp Berea, and continued learning from Mr. Chaffee and all the other staff there. While I learned to water ski, tube, and lots of other things during my summers, the most impactful part of my time at Camp Berea was that first week, and that interaction of love and discipline with Mr. Chaffee. He had demonstrated hard but sincere and redemptive love, and it helped me in the healing process, to see good, godly discipline!

Soccer, academics, popularity, and girls still maintained their place as the four gods in my life though. I had put God on the back burner, and I focused myself on these four idols to fill my time and life. Praise God that He was still active and moving in and through my life, and that He didn't give up on me! Though I was not walking in a daily love relationship with Him, God was still faithful to love and move in me for His glory. The fingerprints of the Potter are evident, even when we don't recognize them, seek Him, nor give credit to Him.

Chapter 13

Forgiveness

On Thursday, February 10th, 1994, God placed another finger-print on my life! That was the evening when I attended a large event with my youth group, as I was 15 years old. A karate sensei was doing a presentation for multiple youth groups. The sensei (a martial art instructor) was a Christian who used his martial arts abilities for God's glory. He demonstrated breaking bricks and wood with his bare hands. It was quite impressive to me to watch his hand gracefully glide through bricks and wood. It almost seemed like a trick, magic, or miracle.

The sensei spoke about how the bricks and wood represent obstacles and distractions, things that block and get in the way of our relationship with God. At the end of the demonstration, he invited the youth to go up front and try breaking a brick or piece of wood with their hands. It was surprising to me that, in a large auditorium filled with so many young people from several youth groups, very few went forward. I was one of the only ones to go up.

I thought I was just going to break some wood from my own strength, due to my underlying anger. The sensei seemed able to do it so easily, and he was not even upset! He asked if I wanted to break a brick or wood, and I selected wood. I quickly hit the block of wood in front of me and my hand stung as it just bounced back at me, leaving the piece of wood undamaged. All I achieved was a red and very sore hand, and a little embarrassment.

The sensei then took me aside and talked with me for a few minutes, before allowing me to try breaking anything else. He got very specific with his questions and wanted to know if I needed to forgive people in my life. After I shared some of my story, he talked to me about the importance of truly forgiving the people from my past, as well as asking forgiveness for myself. He went so far as to show me that the Bible says that, if I do not forgive others, then God will not forgive me (Matthew 6:14–15 NIV). God had given me a keen awareness of my sins, and I was certain that I needed His forgiveness every day, as well as the ability to forgive others. The sensei then told me about the great peace and freedom that comes in the process of forgiveness, which can only truly work when it is connected to God's love. The sensei then explained that there is a proper technique to break an object. He also explained that this proper technique parallels the need for a proper heart condition to truly offer others (and one's self) forgiveness.

The sensei then put the unbroken piece of wood to the side and got out a big brick. He assured me that I could break it if I really wanted to, just as I could really forgive the people of my past if I really wanted to. (Note: I was fully aware God was intervening in this moment and that this was not a mystical formula one must follow to receive forgiveness.) The sensei then explained I should declare forgiveness to the people in my past as I brought my hand, in a tight fist, down and through the brick. Then, as my hand would come out the other side of the brick, I should open it in release of pressure, which would also represent letting go of the weight and pressure of the unforgiveness that I had held onto in my heart. The sensei assured me that in this process of forgiveness, if my heart was genuinely in it, I would find true freedom and peace. With my heart burning with a passion to forgive others, as well as my-self, and a desire to know more of God's great peace and freedom, I approached the brick with the proper technique that the sensei had demonstrated. Astonishing to me, my hand sliced right down through that brick as if it were not even there. The broken brick was then signed by the sensei, and he gave me both pieces, telling me to keep them to remember this moment of victory and forgiveness. That broken 2-piece brick remained in the youth group lounge at my church for all my adolescent years. Though I know not where it is right now, it was an important obstacle to break, and an amazing process to encounter.

In that moment, God granted me the ability to truly forgive all the people from the abuse and vileness of my past, and to forgive myself for my own sinful ways. The moment that I broke the brick God gave me a supernatural gift of freedom and forgiveness. A huge and major weight lifted off of me. God's love has compelled me since then to be on my knees interceding for all the people who abused and neglected me. My prayer is that they might know Him in a true eternity-changing, life-transforming love relationship! There are not enough words to portray the power and awe of that supernatural moment, as the Potter continued molding me into His image. Freeing me to fully forgive others and myself was another marked and pivotal moment, and fingerprint of the Potter, in my first twenty years of life.

Chapter 14

Death Looms

Though God had moved so mightily and generously, I still had Him sitting on a back burner. Despite the fact that I was still reading my Bible, going to church and youth group, and even had head knowledge of God, He was neither the center nor focus of my life. However, the supernatural blessings and moments by which I am now marked by the Potter's fingerprints have no less value. At this time, I was still living for the four gods that I had allowed space in my life—soccer, academics, popularity, and girls. I was a social butterfly and life of the party. I was also excited about the possibility of getting back into a relationship with my first love from a middle school romance, though God had different plans for me.

God is a jealous God, not wanting to share His glory with false gods. We often allow other things in our lives to compete for God's place. He rightfully desires that He would be uncontestably number one, in each of our lives, the One and Only God. God decided to interact supernaturally, miraculously, and intimately in my life at this time, to reprioritize my life and priorities, and to remove the idols of my life.

Three days into my freshman year of high school, was the first weekend of my high school experience. The soccer coach had given us the weekend off, so we had no practices, scrimmages, or games planned. Saturday, September 3rd, 1994 is a date I will never forget—though I have absolutely no memory of anything that took place on that day. The events of that day have been shared to me by many witnesses and participants since then. That Saturday morning, because I am a social butterfly, I was hanging out with a bunch of friends. A decision was made for us to go in to the city, to watch a movie and shop at the mall. As teens, we just wanted to get away from our 'hick' town, and enjoy a day in the city. A father of one of the kids had agreed to drive us to the mall. Since he only had a pickup truck, a few of the kids piled in the front of the truck with him and buckled up, while the rest of us just climbed up in the open back of the pick-up truck. This was not illegal at the time, just a bit unwise and risky.

As we were traveling down a main road, headed for the city, the driver got distracted. I was told later that I may have been the cause of his distraction, as I was trying to get a jacket for one of the girls who was cold. Whatever the cause, somehow the driver got distracted and the pickup swerved off the road going fifty-five miles an hour. The truck then slammed into a tree along the edge of the road. The contact and impact propelled the truck into a 360-degree spin. My body was thrown out over the edge of the truck, and I was then leaning out and holding on for dear life to not to fall out. As the truck continued to spin, my head slammed against the tree. My body immediately went unconscious and I flew out of the back of the truck onto the edge of the road. I slid along the side of the road for more than 30 feet. Most of my clothes were torn off my body as I slid, and when I came to a halt I laid lifeless on the side of the road, as my heart had stopped beating.

Someone immediately dialed 911, and the paramedics were quick to get to the scene. They pronounced me dead, as my heart had stopped, but, all praise to God, they were able to revive me. In the ambulance, on the way to the hospital, my heart stopped a second time, and I was pronounced dead again. All praise to God, the paramedics were able to get my heart beating again. Finally, as we arrived to the emergency room and were entering, my heart stopped yet again. For a third time I was pronounced dead. God was very generous though, in allowing the paramedics to get my heart working again a third time!

Shannon kept a journal from the day of the accident until I was released from the hospital, and in it she wrote about this experience of me being rushed into the emergency room, looking whiter than a ghost. She watched as the paramedics and doctors worked to revive me. I had died three times. However, God, the giver of life, determined it was not my time to depart from this world. Praise God, the Potter, for His hand and fingerprints on my life, and for giving the doctors and paramedics the ability to revive me three times! Once the paramedics had revived me the third time, I entered into a comatose state.

In this accident, I received a Traumatic Closed Head Injury (TCHI) and a Traumatic Brain Injury (TBI). My short-term memory and ability for retention were significantly impaired. I lost one hundred percent of my lower body strength, and seventy percent of my upper body strength. When my head hit the tree, my brain slammed against the left side of my skull causing some permanent brain damage. It also caused an imbalance of strength on my right side of my body, as well as significant internal bleeding, bruising, and swelling inside my head, due to the direct impact.

I suffered through a series of three seizures the night of the accident. Several times, in the first few hours, the doctors were concerned they were going to have to open my skull to alleviate the pressure from my brain swelling. Praise God though, for another fingerprint from the Potter. As the doctors were preparing for surgery, the swelling decreased on its own, and the surgery was cancelled. I remained in a comatose state for six days.

When a person emerges from a coma, it is not with the clarity you and I now have. The process takes time, and there may be several waves of consciousness and unconsciousness never remembered by the patient nor recognized by the doctors. My experience of 'coming to' also included intense pain, in my head and throughout my body. Later, I was told that in my first bout of consciousness (which I do *not* remember) I slurred the word "Soccer."

My first wave of consciousness that I do remember (and is recorded in Shannon's journal) was in my hospital room, which was packed with visitors off to the right of me. I was also informed by Shannon that there was a long line of people out in the hall waiting to see me. The shrill painful sound of the phone ringing, the bright lights, and the people all excited to see my eyes opening were what welcomed me back into the realm of consciousness. I was completely unaware of where I was or why I was there.

Chapter 15

God's Mighty Answer:
Pillar #2

Laying in my hospital bed, I found myself coming into consciousness from my coma, for the first time that I can remember. As I looked around my hospital room, I was amazed at the
outpouring of love from so many people. My heart was swelling
in joy that people seemed to really care about me. It was in that
moment, that God gave me the second pillar of my faith. It was a
moment that truly propelled me from being a man of faith, to being
a man of absolute certainty that God exists and that He loves me!
It was a moment that God, the Potter, used to convey to me how
much He loves *me*! For in that moment, God stepped out beyond
all the boundaries, barriers, doubts, and disbeliefs I might have had
towards Him, and He broke into time and space. God Almighty
audibly spoke three sentences directly and specifically to me, that
are now indelibly imprinted on my heart, mind, and soul for all
eternity. God, the Potter, said to me . . .

> *"Look around you, and see that you are loved!"*

This was God's first audibly spoken sentence to me; one
which carries great significance for me. All my life I had longed for

someone to love and care about me. God was intentionally showing me that He had placed me in the midst of people who really loved and cared about me. It was incredible to feel the love of others all around me!

God's second sentence to me consisted of just five small words, but they are the five hugest, most powerful, life-changing words in all of history, especially when spoken directly from the mouth of The Potter! These five words, directly from the mouth of God to me, are what hold me, mold me, make me, and carry me each and every day! God, the Potter, said to me . . .

"Know that I love you!"

Hearing those words, directly from the mouth of God, has sustained and nurtured me every day of my life since He spoke them to me. I wanted to know that I could be loved, and God not only showed me others around me who loved me, but also spoke directly to me of His own love for me! What an indescribably powerful experience to hear God, Himself, proclaim that He loves me! Those are my five most favorite words ever! From that moment forward I have never doubted. I know that He loves me!

God's third and final audible sentence to me was . . .

"See this as an answer to prayer!"

Those words have given me profound certainty that God hears me as I pray, and, though His timing is very different from ours (and in my perspective is quite slow), He answers according to His will, in His perfect plan and timing. God answers prayers!

I can now go confidently before Him in prayer, knowing that He hears me, trusting Him to reply in His way and timing. Communication is critical for any relationship to be successful, and God desires communication with His children. Over time, my prayers have matured and grown to be more for the things of His heart, instead of just mine. Of this, though, I am certain, God does answer prayers! I am certain that He allowed this accident, and even ordained it, at a time when I was not walking intentionally in a love relationship with Him. He used the accident to get my attention, and used His words of love as a fingerprint upon me to capture my heart.

Now I find it important to remind you of my very first prayer request that I prayed when I was seven years old, shortly after I received Jesus Christ as my Savior. After having seen classmates and teachers care for me when I was physically hurt, I had decided to seek the greatest hurt in my life to see who would really show up and care. In my prayer, I asked God for three things. First, I asked to be in a car accident, and God eventually granted it. Secondly, I asked for death, and God granted it. Yet, His eventual purpose for my life must have been more than what had been accomplished in the first fifteen years of my life, since He allowed me to be revived back to life. The third, and the most significant aspect of my prayer, was to see if someone would show up and sincerely express concern and care for me, that someone could really love me. In so many ways, He also answered this part!

God is so faithful. He answered my first prayer exactly and yet so very differently from the way I had prayed and asked Him to, and for that I am eternally grateful! As I laid in the hospital bed and looked at all the visitors, it was evident most of the people cared enough about me that they would have been present at my funeral, had I not been brought back to life! God had completely answered my prayer, and He accomplished so much more than just a simple answered prayer through that accident. He spoke directly to me! He convinced me that He saw, heard, knew, and loved me! Even more amazing, in that moment I became convinced that He would always speak with me, see me, know me, and love me! It is a supernatural certainty, when you hear the audible voice of God, that transforms you from just believing to being absolutely certain!

These three sentences propelled my relationship with Jesus forward, and are an amazing fingerprint of God on my life. It was in that moment, right after God spoke directly to me, that I made the greatest, hardest, most beneficial, and yet most costly commitment of my life. I, in that moment, made a life-long commitment to God, at the age of fifteen, while lying in that hospital bed, that I would go wherever He calls me, and do whatever He asks of me . . . no matter where, what, when, how, or why . . . so long as He would call me clearly! I would always serve and follow Him no matter what the cost! This was the moment that I surrendered my life to God's

Lordship; when I came to know Him as both my Savior AND my Lord! Over the years, I have kept that promise and as a result I have been tremendously blessed. God has been very clear with me, and I have been amazed at where and how He calls me!

I must elaborate here. Many people profess to know Jesus Christ as Savior. I boldly declare it is not sufficient to just receive the gift of salvation from God. He also wants, and rightfully deserves, to have authority, and the ability to direct and guide our lives, as our Lord. My Lordship commitment to The Potter has been the hardest and costliest commitment of my life, but it has also been the most rewarding. I challenge you to let Jesus Christ be the Lord of your life! Accept His gift of salvation and let Him be Savior, but don't stop there! Allow Him to lead you and have authority over your life, as your Lord, and your life will be used by the hand of The Potter in ways you have never imagined!

Chapter 16

Why Do Bad Things Happen?

Many people ask the question, "If God is really good, then why does He allow bad things to happen to good people?" I am not naïve, and definitely would never classify myself as a 'good' person, because the Bible clearly states there is no one good, not even one (Psalms 14:2–3 NIV). However, if we entertain the question, and allow ourselves for just a moment to incorrectly believe that somehow, I am a 'good' person, I believe my accident can shed some light on the answer.

The first reason why this 'bad' thing happened to my so-called 'good' person was because God wanted to use the accident as an answer to my first prayer request. It was a profound experience in seeing and knowing that God really does hear and respond to our prayers. While He doesn't always answer our prayer in our time frame, nor in the way we desire or expect, He is faithful to answer our prayers. The Potter used this answered prayer greatly to increase my desire to pray even more, and not just for myself, but for so many others as well! Many people have been blessed because God allowed this 'bad' thing to happen to this 'good' person.

The second reason God allowed this 'bad' thing to happen to my so-called 'good' person was to show me there are those who care about me and love me. Far more importantly, He used the accident as an opportunity to intimately share His own love for me . . . "Know that I love you!" I would take a thousand 'bad' things in my life if each were accompanied with the voice of God expressing His overwhelming love!

A third reason why God allows 'bad' things to happen to so-called 'good' people is because what we perceive as bad may be necessary to produce the growth and change God desires. An analogy to clarify what I mean is the picture of the human muscle. As someone who has tried to work out and take seriously God's call for us to honor Him with our body, I am aware of the muscles in my body.

When someone intentionally works out to increase the size of their muscles, they must push themselves to a point known as 'the burn'. If you've ever experienced this, you know the term can be descriptive of an intense pain. This burning sensation is the result of microscopic tears occurring in the muscle. It is through the healing process of those torn muscles that leads to increasing muscle strength and mass. Some might perceive 'the burn' as a bad thing, but serious body builders and health fitness professionals know the pain is required to build size and strength. I see this accident as 'the burn' that caused me to grow and increase in Christ a whole lot! God used this accident to reprioritize Himself as my first, and only, God.

For the fourth reason why 'bad' things happen to 'good' people, I need to share a true story of a business man who, at the time of my accident, was struggling spiritually. He, his wife, and his daughter had been going to church and living a nominal Christian life, but recently the wife and daughter had begun walking in an intentional love relationship with Jesus. The husband, on the other hand, was resistant to surrender his life to Jesus Christ. It felt uncomfortable to have to give some things up on Sundays, to be at church, and to have to give up some ways of life that didn't align with God's desire.

On the morning of September 3rd, 1994 in a town near where I lived, this business man started his busy day by having breakfast with his wife and daughter. Then he went to his car to get his brief-case, to review some documents for a meeting he had scheduled for later that day. As he opened his car door, the car phone between the seats caught his eye. (Yes, this took place back in the dark ages before our current addiction to mobile cellular phones.) For months, the man had intended to go through the necessary steps to activate 911 on his car phone, but he just never seemed to have the time. Despite his busy schedule, he chose this particular Saturday morning to intentionally figure out how to activate his 911 service. Having researched how to do so, the man activated the 911 service on his car phone, before reviewing the necessary documents for his upcoming meeting.

Shortly after finishing up some paper work and heading off to his appointment, that man found himself following a pickup truck filled with several teenagers riding in the back. He watched as the driver became distracted and swerved off the road, and ultimately straight into a tree. He then quickly swerved to miss a body (my body) which was flung from the back of the truck. He pulled off the road, grabbed his car phone shakenly, and dialed 911 to report the accident.

As this business man sat trembling, he knew it was no coinci-dence he had just enabled 911 on his car phone that morning. He truly sensed Jesus pulling at his heart. He knew that there had been divine intervention; God trying to get his attention. There, on the side of the road, waiting for the ambulance to arrive, that man gave up all his resistance, and he surrendered his heart and life to Jesus Christ as Savior and Lord!

The reason I can tell you of this man's conversion and sur-render to Jesus Christ is because I got to meet him about a year after my accident. I was on a youth group outing at a local YMCA, where several youth groups met for a game night. After limitedly playing basketball and soccer, I went into the men's locker room to change up to swim in the pool. In the locker room, I noticed a man sitting on a bench staring at me. He asked if my name was J.R., and I told him yes. He asked me if something traumatic had happened to me close to a year before that specific time. Again, I responded yes. He then proceeded to explain how God had used the accident that I had been in to claim his heart and life for God's kingdom! I was overwhelmed to realize that through the accident, the loving hand of the Potter was extended to someone I had never known and his life was eternally changed. This deeply touched my heart! We joyfully cried together, and I hugged a new brother in the kingdom of God! This was another great fingerprint of God, and not just on my life, but visibly upon the life of others as well!

I have given four positive reasons why I believe God allowed this 'bad' thing to happen to a 'good' person. However, there is a fifth reason that is not so positive, but I don't feel it would be fair for me not to include it. Sometimes God allows 'bad' things to happen just because He has offered us free will, and will not always intervene to make everything happy-go-lucky good. The consequences of free will can often be painful and negative. While my heart may have been to help one of the girls with us to not be cold, it was not wise to lean around to the front window and distract the driver. Sometimes God allows 'bad' things to happen to 'good' people, solely because it is the natural consequence of poor decisions and actions. We are not puppets, nor are we yet in paradise. A good parent allows for their child to experience some errors and falls on their own, though they may be preventable, because, in the child getting back up and learning the consequences of their decisions and actions, they can continue to grow and mature.

I really do love when people ask, "If God is really good, why does He allow bad things to happen to good people?" I have so many examples to share from my life where God has taken bad, even tragic, situations and turned them into good. We may not always understand why God is allowing bad things to happen, but I have come to a place where I am absolutely certain that God is using those bad things to grow people and accomplish His purpose. I can fully trust that His allowing 'bad' things to happen does have a good outcome somehow down the road.

Now to summarize, God allowed this 'bad' thing to happen to 'good' ole me for at least four positive reasons. The first was because it was an answer to my first prayer request. God showed me that He does answer our prayers, in His timing and in His way, all for His glory. It deepened my belief in the power of being on my knees (in prayer) before God, as well as my practice to do so, not only speaking to Him but also listening for His voice and direction.

Secondly, God used this 'bad' thing as an opportunity to reveal to me that people love me, as well as to share His own love for me. God had clearly and audibly spoken the five most amazing words of my life, directly to me; *"Know that I love you!"*

A third positive reason why God allowed this 'bad' thing to happen to me was to grow and strengthen me in many ways—the first of which was (and is) my relationship with Him! He removed my four idols, and reprioritized Himself in my life as my One and Only God! He also developed my perseverance and will to continue forward, and to do good to, and for, others. God, the Potter, used the accident as transforming and growing time in my life, to form the vessel that I was more into the vessel that He wants for me to be.

The fourth positive reason why God allowed my accident (a 'bad' thing) to happen was because, in His perfect timing, He knew exactly what it would take to break the resistance of a business man, and to increase the population of the kingdom of heaven. Thus, God, the Potter, used my accident as a fingerprint on eternity! He did not only have me in mind, but used the accident as an opportunity to invite someone else into His hands, to be formed and molded by Him! God increased the number of family members of heaven through the accident!

Chapter 17

Reprioritizing and Removing

Hearing God tell me personally of His love for me was more than enough to reprioritize Him as my number one focus, and my only God! However, He left no chance for me to immediately run back to the four gods that I had begun to serve: soccer, academics, popularity, and girls. He did, however, promise to restore each of those areas in due time, in a way that would be healthy, good, and bring honor to Him.

As a result of the accident, my ability to walk, to speak, and to write were greatly diminished; requiring extensive physical, occupational, motor skills, and speech therapy. Obviously, soccer went right out the door, as the brain injuries, deaths, and seizures that I had suffered were of great concern for the doctors. They were adamant that hitting my head with the soccer ball, or against anyone or anything else for that matter, would be incredibly dangerous, to the extent that they cautioned that I could die if I refused their medical advice. Therefore, soccer was removed from my life, at least for a period of time.

I remember a meeting that was held with all the doctors, therapists, and even the foster parents and Shelly, while I was still in the hospital. The neurologists concluded that, due to the brain damage I had received, I would most likely not be able to complete high school, never be able to play soccer again, nor would I be able to ever run again. I will never forget the thud of my heart as I heard the doctors say that I may never be able to run again. I immediately decided that they were wrong, and set a personal goal that one day I would run a full marathon as an act of worship, if God would give me my legs back. I committed to running the marathon with my hands lifted high in praise and worship to God, if He would enable me to run again.

One strategy I employed to learn how to walk/run again, at least while hospitalized, was to try chasing the nurses while using my walker. It was just to be funny, but really did help motivate me to force my legs back into use. The nurses and staff also got a kick out of it. Recovering my leg strength was a slow process, but it did enable me to run again. God had answered my prayer to let me run again. Just two years after the accident, one of my high school coaches timed me running my personal record for a mile; four minutes and fifty-nine seconds. Several years later, on May 31, 2009, I would run my first ever full marathon, the San Diego Rock 'n Roll Marathon, and I ran all 26.2 miles. My time was not as good as I wanted, as I did it in 4:52:04, due to an unexpected knee injury, but, as I painfully hobbled to the finish line, my arms and hands were lifted high in worship to God!

Due to my head injury, soccer could no longer be a professional pursuit, much less a high school sport, but God had graciously allowed me to still enjoy playing some sports for fun, after I had received significant healing. Much later on, in 2004, I joined a missional soccer team headed by a youth pastor of a Pennsylvanian church to travel to Portugal! Portugal was the host nation of the United European Futbol Association's EuroCup soccer championship in 2004. At the request of the chaplain of the EuroCup, the Pennsylvanian youth pastor put together a mission soccer team, and he took us to Portugal to play soccer against professionals, retired professionals, and the Portuguese Army! With each group we got to share the gospel, and I had the opportunity to share the amazing story of God's great faithfulness in my life! I am humbled at how the Potter used my life, my love for soccer, and my testimony to grow the kingdom of heaven, as some of those who heard my testimony in person accepted Jesus Christ as Savior and Lord!

When the doctors also told me that I might never complete high school, due to the severity of my brain injuries, I was determined that they would be proven wrong. However, for me to succeed, I would need God's miraculous and faithful intervention. To perform well academically, it is imperative to have short term memory and retention, and these had both been greatly diminished in the accident. After the accident, I went from being at the top of my class to struggling to be a C+ student. Academics were certainly something I could no longer serve as a god, or receive attention from. Rather, my studies became a tedious procedure to just get myself to the graduation platform. I needed a tutor, and extended time using repetition, to learn things slowly. However, by God's grace, I graduated. Then God carried me on to pursue and complete a Bachelor's degree in Christian Ministries, and then a Master's degree in Cross-Cultural Studies. Although I still have some difficulty with my memory, God gave me back the ability to learn and pursue higher education, beyond just my high school degree. He also allowed me to maintain my love of learning. He still slowly is healing my memory and the brain injuries. The Potter's fingerprints and faithfulness are great upon my life!

After the accident, popularity and girls were no longer gods in my life either, primarily because my priorities had greatly shifted. I was still a teenager with raging hormones, so it would be a lie to say that I was not at all interested in the girls around me. They just did not have the same focus of my attention that they had had previously. Popularity did not matter to me anymore, though I did have success in high school of developing several good friendships, and was involved in many different extra-curricular groups. I also had some circles of friends in church groups and communities outside of high school.

The accident had significantly changed me, though much more because of hearing God's audible voice than because of any brain damage. Encountering God, in the intimate and tangible, transforms a human being. I was by no means perfect (nor will I ever be until I am in the presence of God in all of eternity), but I was definitely changed. My priorities and desires aligned so much more with God, after hearing His voice, and learning personally and directly from Him of His love for me! I was learning to love people better, more like Jesus.

People all around me had a hard time understanding these changes that had taken place, though. Not only had my life been changed by the awesome love and presence of God, but I also struggled through many black-outs and strange physical side-affects long after the accident. These changes caused a strain and alienation in many of my former friendships and relationships. However, God provided me with new friends and relationships, that were more focused on Him and His Kingdom. He has, since then, carried me throughout the world to share His love, and I have made many friends. I no longer desire popularity, but rather greatly enjoy genuine community and fellowship.

Chapter 18

A Man with No Family

While I was still recovering in the hospital from the car accident, a decision was made that Anne and Kate would be moved out of Shannon and Willy's home, into independent living plans; living in a government owned house in a nearby city. There were some specific issues involved that brought about this decision, and they were practical and realistic. However, at the time, I was very upset with this decision, and I did not understand. I worried for Anne and Kate, because I was not aware if either of them truly recognized the abusive cycle that we had lived in, nor their dire need of Jesus Christ as Lord and Savior. Within just a few months from when they were moved out, both girls became pregnant out of wedlock, and I feared they were going to repeat the cycle of abuse and depravity that we had most unfortunately come from.

After my release from the hospital, I tried for two years to be the best brother I could be. I called Anne and Kate often, but they would not take, nor return, my calls. I would travel to the city where they lived to visit with them, but they refused to see me or would not pay much attention to me at all. I prayed a lot for them, and wished that somehow, we could be close. Finally, when I was seventeen years old, I received a phone call from Kate.

I remember being handed the phone that hung on the wall, with its long spirally cord. I stretched the cord and entered around the corner into the bathroom, shut the door most of the way, and then sat on the toilet with its seat down. Kate proceeded to tell me that, if I really wanted to be a good brother to her and Anne, I would need to get rid of "all the God-crap" in my life. My second greatest passion in all of life is to have a wife and family, but even they will never be able to get me to compromise on God being the center and number one in my life! I tried to explain to Kate that I wanted to love her and Anne as their brother, and to do it with the love of God. Kate hung up the phone on me before I could finish, and I sat there crying, feeling crushed, and like I had just lost the last connection to anything remotely close to actual family.

Over the next few weeks, God did one of the hardest things He has ever done in my life. He convinced me, through His Word and through other believers, that through the accident He had removed almost everything that I had allowed to distract me from having Him as my one true God, as my Savior and Lord. He had removed the four idols. He was now removing the final attachment in life that could compete for His place in my life.

In those next few weeks, God convinced me that He was taking any sense of family away from my life, along with everything else I had so greatly esteemed, valued, and treasured. Anne and Kate were the last connection to any sort of 'real' family. God was calling me to come out and be separate for His purposes and glory. Though it was incredibly hard, I heard Him, believed Him, trusted Him, and was faithful to His call. I let go of all connections to family in my heart and life, trusting that God had a purpose and plan to fulfill with this as well.

God was gracious and personal with me, in this time. He made it very clear that His call for me to come out and be separate was not a punishment, nor a way to remove pleasure from my life. His desire was, and is, for my life to be focused on Him. His call on my life came with a promise. He promised that one day He would bless me with a large and godly family. In Luke 18:29, and in several other passages as well, Jesus says whoever leaves home, brothers, parents, etc., for His sake will receive many times what they have left here on earth, and even more in eternity to come. Though it has not been easy, I have been faithful to His call, not for the rewards, but because He is God and I love and trust Him, and as my Lord, I have committed to obey Him.

God has been faithful with His promise, and I have been greatly blessed by stepping out in faith and being separate for His purposes and glory. God has also been faithful to give back most of the things He removed in an effort to draw me to Him. He has done it in ways so much better than I would ever have been able to design or imagine, with His fingerprints all over my story. I am certain that the Potter will complete His purposes and fulfill all His promises.

Chapter 19

He Knows My Name!

It took me several weeks to internalize and accept the fact that God had removed even family from my life, to make Himself my One and Only God! After those challenging weeks though, when God finally convinced me that He had removed everything from me, so that I would be totally dependent on Him, He then gave me a very precious gift. It was a gift that He had promised me back when I was just seven years old . . . He gave me a new name! He was bringing a blessing upon my life, rather than the curse that had been there from birth! He knows and chose my name, and was ready for me to now receive it!

A sweet lady named Faith, from the church I attended, had been praying for me for a while, and encouraging me a lot in my own growth and faith. One Sunday morning, Faith came to me with a list of names that she felt God had led her to write down from the Bible. The list was made up of names starting with the letters J and R, since J.R. were the initials I was known by in Maine. She shared with me that she had sensed a release from God, that week, to give me the list. She promised to keep praying with me for God's revelation. As I looked at the list, in a spirit of prayer and discernment, two names popped off the paper to my eyes, as if they were highlighted specifically for me . . . Jesse Rivers. In prayerful discernment, God then revealed to me what my true full name is, Jesse Alan Rivers; not the curse of a name placed on me at birth, but rather a name that He has promised to have etched on His hand and marked in the Book of Life for all eternity.

> *See, I have engraved you on the palms of my hands . . .*
> Isaiah 49:16 (NIV)

> *The one who is victorious will, like them, be dressed in white. I will never blot out the name of that person from the book of life, but will acknowledge that name before my Father and his angels.*
> Revelation 3:5 (NIV)

To change my name legally, I had to go through the Maine court system. I waited until I was eighteen years old, so that I could be my own legal representation. No lawyer could know nor understand the importance of this name change as much as I did, and I knew I could best share my case and reasoning with the judge. Therefore, once I was 18 years old, I petitioned the court system for a court hearing to make my name change official and legal. They responded and appointed me a set date for my hearing.

The court is required to publish all court hearings in the local newspaper, prior to the hearing date, so that the public is made aware and able to contest or support the matter. A few weeks prior to my court date of June 17th, 1997 an announcement was placed in the local paper announcing the date and time of my hearing. Almost immediately, Anne, Kate, and Shelly made it known to my social worker that they were going to contest my name change. We no longer had any direct contact or communication. My social worker informed me of their decision to contest my name change, and I began to pray. I was not worried though, because God had clearly shared with me that He was giving me this new name!

As the time approached for the hearing, a life-skills worker from the DHS, who we will call Matt, who had helped me develop some practical abilities and life skills, contacted me. He had heard that I was going to change my name. Matt was excited for me, and told me that he would like to give me a ride and go with me, to my court hearing, as a friend and supporter. I gladly accepted, as I was unable to drive myself, because I had had three seizures the night of my accident, and had to go three years seizure free before I would be allowed to drive. At this time it seemed that there was stronger opposition to me changing my name, than there was support, so I was very thankful that Matt offered me the ride, as well as his friendship and support.

Matt picked me up on the morning of my court hearing, and he drove us to the courthouse. Upon arriving, I was ushered into the court room before the judge. I looked right at the judge, as I shared from my heart about my past, and gave the reasons that I believed it to be necessary to change my name legally. The judge listened intently, got teary eyed, and, as I finished, he banged his gavel and said, "From this day forward, you shall now be officially known as Jesse Alan Rivers." In that moment, I felt the burden and curse of a name that was not my own lift off me! A promise and another fingerprint of God had just been placed upon my life. The joy was incredible! My name was changed! This blessing and promise of God was upon me!

Matt was also excited that I had won my case, and he suggested that we go out and celebrate! After leaving the courthouse in his car, we came to a stop at the first traffic light, as it was red. On the opposite side of that traffic light, in the first oncoming car, sat Shelly, Anne, and Kate. Obviously, they were heading to the courthouse to contest my name being changed, but somehow, they had been delayed. This was yet another fingerprint of God on my life, as He had somehow miraculously delayed them, and thus prevented them from contesting the change of my name. Praise the Potter for His mighty hand! Shelly, Anne, and Kate did not see us, and Matt and I continued on to a place to get some food and celebrate together!

God had chosen my name, given me my name, and then He enabled me to get it legally changed! Knowing that it was now legal, and that it also has been written upon God's hand and in the Eternal Book of Life, I was, and am, elated by the clear name and identity God continues to affirm in me! I love my name . . . Jesse Alan Rivers!

He Knows My Name!

Ever since God gave me my new and real name, I have come up with a little song that I often sing to myself (usually in the shower because I do not have the greatest singing voice). The main line in the song gets repeated often, because it is an incredible and life-altering truth for me! I'll spare you from hearing me sing it, but here are the words:

> He knows my name!
> He knows my name!
> He knows my name!
> He chose me as I am!
> Loves me just the same!
> He knows my name!
> He chose my name!
> He knows my name!

Chapter 20

JAR

Jesse Alan Rivers . . . JAR

 God has woven so much meaning and purpose into this incredible gift of a name, which He has given me. I did not recognize much of the significance, symbolism, or truth that God had crafted into it, until after I had legally changed it. God has taken His time in revealing many of the intricacies and hidden meanings. In fact, at first, I even argued with Him over one specific aspect of the name.

 At first, I wanted to spell Alan with two Ls and an E because I believed that *Allen* was a stronger and more masculine way to spell it. Praise God for His persistence and purposes, as I sensed that it would be disobedient if I did not accept the *Alan* spelling! I am now so thankful that I did receive my middle name, *Alan*, just as God desired for me to! The following will explain some of the meaning behind each of my names, and why I am so blessed by God's way of spelling *Alan*.

 J.A.R. . . . The initials of my name stand for an acronym that will never fade away, though my name very well may fade away and be forgotten in time. J.A.R. stands for Jesus Always Rules. This truth will always exist and can never be destroyed or stripped away. J.A.R. also spells out the word *jar*, and I am a jar, a vessel in the hands of the Potter . . . that He has molded, is molding, and will continue to mold and use for His glory. The multitude of God's fingerprints on my life are evidence of His hand molding and shaping me and my life circumstances, to be used for His glory. JAR . . . A vessel in the hands of the Potter!

Jesse . . . Jesse is the biblically historical father of the great King David. Jesse had a large and godly family; a lineage that traces all the way to Jesus; whom the Bible refers to as the Root and Branch of Jesse. As God gave me this great name, He also gave me a great promise that my family line will also be a large and godly family. I am walking in faith of this promise. Having recently gotten married (which you can read about in a future book I'll write, God-willing), God has started fulfilling this promise. Me and my wife are also hoping to experience the joys of being God-fearing parents to many children, in God's timing and guidance!

Jesse . . . Jesse originates as a Hebrew word. The meaning of Jesse in Hebrew is the fullest testimony of my life, for Jesse in Hebrew means "God is!" or "God exists!" After hearing the voice of God, and knowing His love and presence in my life, I know there is no greater reality or truth than God Himself. This is a truth I am committed to making known every day of my life, in any opportunity God grants for me to share it. I know that *God exists!* and that *God is!* He is my King, Redeemer, Savior, Father, Lord, Friend, God, Potter, and so much more! God is! God exists!

Alan . . . When I got to college, I found out why God had specifically chosen Alan as my middle name. A dear friend of mine found the definition for the specific spelling, *Alan,* and it stands for "little rock." I was quite pleased with this definition, as it seemed strong to me, and I know that God is the Big Rock. God also, later on, revealed to me, in greater significance, how I am to be a "little rock."

It happened approximately seven years after I had accepted God's name for me legally. While I was sitting in a small country Pennsylvanian church one Sunday morning, intently listening to a pastor preach a convicting sermon, God interrupted. It is not as if I was just daydreaming, though! This pastor, who was preaching that Sunday, is one of my favorite preachers. He preached messages that are challenging and convicting to the body of Christ, that we would become more of who God intends for us to be. I was thoroughly engrossed in his message this specific Sunday morning, when God decided to interrupt. I am not sure where you stand, or what you believe, with the supernatural acts of God, but I know and experience God's supernatural interaction in my life regularly. In that moment, God interrupted my focus and gave me a vision. The vision is still as stark and clear for me today, as it was that moment when God placed it upon me.

The vision starts with an aerial view, as I am looking down upon (or hovering over) a very dark space. I am moving forward until I am able to see a very large and dark rock way out in front of me, below me. The vision is a mix of dark shades of gray and black, and is very dark and uninviting. This rock that I now see is massive. I am not talking the size of a soccer ball, a building, nor even of a sky-scraper or city. This rock is more like the size of an entire continent.

This rock proceeds up out of the water from the left to the right, and the left face of the rock climbs at a staggering incline. The front face of the rock is completely vertical, as are the back face, and right-side face. The rock is wide, with all sides of it impossible to climb all the way to the top. The rock has a small flat ridge along the top that extends the entire width of the rock, from the front face of the rock to the back face. The edge of the ridge, on the right side of the rock, is a jagged cliff face that drops all the way back down to the water. The rock is extending up out of a dark, raging sea. There are whitecaps all around, as the sea is violently moving.

As I am in this vision, I seem to move closer toward the massive rock. I suddenly see that the rough water around the rock is full of people. Some are trying to climb up the cliffs to get away from the pounding and crashing waves. Others are floundering and flailing. Some are pushing others under to hold themselves up. Some have found that floating on their backs is a great way to keep their heads above water. It is clear that, for survival, the goal is to reach the ridge atop the massive rock. Yet none are being successful in any of their endeavors to reach the top of the rock.

I am then taken to the top of the rock, hovering above the flat ridge. As I am brought closer, there is suddenly a huge burst and contrast in color from everything else in the vision that is dark and dreary. On the top of the rock is a tropical paradise. There are all types of colors, fluorescent and bright, as well as beautiful vibrant bushes and flowers of all imaginable types and sizes. Upon the ridge is an amazing sense of warmth, peace, joy, and tranquility. The bright vibrant paradise atop the rock is emanating a brilliant light and warmth, while everything else in the vision is so dark, damp, and cold.

While in this vision, God revealed to me that the rock and sea represent the tumultuous and trying human life, and the human journey to find peace, truth, and God Himself. The waves of the water, the cliffs, and the darkness represent Satan, evil, flesh, self, and all that pulls humanity away from seeking and trusting God, and all that causes us to focus on how to save ourselves through self-preservation. At the top of the rock, the paradise represents eternal salvation and a never-ending love relationship with God.

In the vision, God then brings me back to the front face of the rock. As I am nearing the rock, I now can see a thin trail that runs up the entire rock in a slight crack and indentation. This trail travels all the way from the raging sea at the base of the rock up to the flat ridge atop the rock. As I get closer, I see that the thin trail is also emitting a vibrant florescent yellow and green light and a gentle warmth, in contrast to the dark and cold rock and sea all around it. The trail represents the only way to get to the top and to receive salvation; a personal love relationship with Jesus Christ. It is the only path and way to the top, and it can only be walked with Him. In the Bible, John 14:6 NIV, Jesus states, "I am the way, and the truth, and the life. No one comes to the Father, except through me." Jesus is the trail!

In the vision, God then brings me to the base of the front face of the rock, where that trail meets the water. Here the water is pounding against the rock base with a relentless force. At the base of the rock, in the water near the beginning of this trail, sits a little rock. If people try to just stand atop this little rock, they are not safe. Waves are dangerously crashing over it and this little rock has no power to save, brighten, or warm the people. However, it is in a pivotal location to be a stepping stone to help the people get onto the only path to the top of the rock.

In that moment God so generously and gently whispered to me, 'You are that little rock.' Though I have no power to save anyone, nor can I prevent the waves of life from crashing in and around me nor them, I can and will be the little rock that is a stepping stone to help people find the only trail; a love relationship with Jesus, that will take them up the steep and dark rock, the journey of life, to reach the paradise, eternal salvation with God, at the top. I am that little rock, and I will share Jesus Christ with as many as will listen and receive. *Alan* means 'little rock' and I praise God He has made me a little rock for His glory!

Rivers . . . Rivers are steady, fast-flowing bodies of water. A remarkable thing about a river is the power it possesses to overcome obstacles in its way. In the confrontation between a river and a rock, the river always wins . . . not because it is bigger, stronger, nor more solid, but because it is persistent and consistent. It will wear away the rock, make a path around the rock, or just push up and move over the rock. It may get slowed down and pushed back, but the river will consistently pick up and move forward. God revealed to me that I am a river that has faced many rocks and obstacles, and that I have consistently and persistently picked up and moved forward wearing them away, moving over them, or passing around them all.

However, for a river to take glory for its persistence and consistence would be wrong. For me, this river that I am, it would also be wrong for me to take glory for myself. For any river to be able to overcome a rock and/or obstacle, it must continually move forward. To be able to do so, it must have a main body of water, a main source that replenishes it and keeps it moving forward. That is true also in this Rivers' life! God has been the main source to replenish me and keep me moving forward for His glory, overcoming all obstacles!

It was hard for most people who knew me from Maine to call me anything other than J.R. That is okay with me though, because I believe God has created this as a reminder of where He has brought me from, and to give encouragement and hope for where He is now leading and guiding me. In the Bible we can read of God directing Joshua to have twelve Israelites gather stones of remembrance from the riverbed of the Jordan, as God parted it, so that they would not forget the hardship of the past and His great work and blessing in their life to bring them into the promised land of milk and honey (Joshua 4:1–7 NIV). People say to forget the past, but I do believe God has allowed me to remain known by some as J.R. so that I will never forget what He has rescued me from, and where He has brought me to! I know that I am a J.A.R. in the hands of the Potter, and I am so thankful and blessed for this name that He has given me.

I would like to share one final note regarding the change in my name. In the last several years, another important aspect and revelation about my name has been revealed to me. God has led me to be an advocate for orphaned, abandoned, abused, vulnerable, and homeless children of Latin America. Much of this region speaks Spanish, and it is amazing to me that, only with the spelling of *Alan* as God chose and directed so many years ago, with one L and an A, my whole name can be translated into Spanish! My name in Spanish is Isai Alan Rios (Eesighee Alan Reeoos)! So, when God gave me my name, He already knew my future destination, and was giving me a name that would work well for that location too! Praise God, the Potter, for all the ways He has His fingerprints and His hand upon my life, including even my name!

Chapter 21

Mission and Challenges

At the time that God spoke directly to me of His love for me, when I was fifteen years old, He also began guiding and directing me toward missions and advocacy for, and ministry to, children. In 1997, the summer before my senior year of high school, my youth group was planning a mission trip to Mexico, and I felt God directing me to go on the trip. To be honest, I was a little concerned that He might call me into full-time ministry or missions, and selfishly, I was reluctant. I made a bargain with Him though, thinking I would be able to dissuade Him from calling me to lifelong mission and ministry. I told God that I would pay in full my first mission trip just this once. If He expected me to travel in mission anywhere else, He would have to provide the money. I felt pretty clever in this deal I was making, but I am sure that God just chuckled. I joined my youth group on the Mexico mission trip, and there I fell in love with three precious children, whom I still pray for to this day . . . Meli (*Maylee*), Deli (*Daylee*), and Alejandro. God really drew my heart to those precious children, and, though our team did lots of manual labor and work on the trip, I experienced such a joy in loving on those kids, and helping them to know God better.

After my accident and hearing God's voice, I had made the commitment to Him that I would go anywhere and do anything that He would ask of me, as long as He clearly directed me. While I was on this mission trip to La Paz and La Purisima, Mexico, with my youth group, God reminded me of that commitment I had made to Him, and I sensed He was testing me to see if I would honor my commitment. He won. Sure enough, on that trip I recommitted myself to go anywhere, at any time, if God would just call me clearly, all for His glory.

It was around that same time when God gave also me my life verses, which I continually try to live out:

> *Trust in the Lord with all your heart and lean not on your*
> *own understanding; in all your ways acknowledge Him,*
> *and He will make your paths straight.*
> Proverbs 3: 5–6 (NIV)

I have now been in more than thirty-five countries throughout the world serving God. My heart and life are mission focused, and what a joy it is to see others accept the awesome gift of salvation and the love relationship God so generously and freely offers!

Returning to Maine after the mission trip to Mexico, I started thinking about college applications. Unbeknownst to me, the DHS had evaluated my case independently from anyone else's, because of the special involvement I had in advocacy for the children within the state of Maine DHS system. Throughout my time in state custody, I saw that many people had a negative stereotype and misperception about children in state custody or in the foster care system. (Here I need to note that I distinguish between children in state custody and children in foster care. There are children in state custody who cannot be in foster care, for any number of reasons, and may need to live in group homes, individual living plans, etc., but every child in foster care is also a child in state custody. I lived in foster care and was in state custody.)

Many people seemed to think that children in foster care or in state custody are just wastes and drains on society, and believed they would only end up being thieves, murderers, rapists, and the scum of society. Rather than being critical about people's poor perceptions though, I decided to take a positive approach and prove them wrong. I was also aware of some problems within the state custody system, and once again, instead of complaining, I decided to help form a panel of youth who were in state custody. We joined together in becoming part of the solution rather than the problem.

The youth panel did some great work to improve the image of foster care kids, and other children in state's custody as well. We worked with the commissioner of the Department of Human Services, the state governor, a congressman, and several other people working for the state government. We were involved in training new social workers, organizing a youth rally for the children in state's custody, and influencing the state regarding the financial aid that foster care youth received for schooling. Our panel also did extensive research into questions and answers for children entering into state custody—including an explanation of rights, services, and benefits. Our findings were compiled and put into publication as the first handbook ever created by youth—for youth in state custody. I was passionate for these children to not be known by stereotypes, false accusations, and/or poor labels, but that they might be given a chance to thrive, succeed, and break the stigmas and stereotypes that they so often encountered. I already knew that I, myself, would also break those preconceived perceptions of me, as one who was a child in foster care/state custody.

After the state of Maine DHS considered my contributions, as well as my determination to succeed in life, they offered me an ideal situation. They were willing to pay for me to go to any state college in Maine, all-expenses paid with a little spending money as well! Though this definitely was a situation one could not just pass up, I clearly sensed God was asking me to trust Him and surrender the future of my education to Him. (If you can recall . . . one of the gods in my life before the accident was academics.)

Towards the end of that summer, before my senior year of high school, I visited a friend, Eric, at Messiah College (now Messiah University), located near Harrisburg, Pennsylvania. Eric was the son of the pastor from the church I had attended when I accepted Jesus as my Savior. We had built a strong friendship and brotherly love throughout our teenage years. He was having a weekend getaway to a cabin in the woods with some friends, and he had invited me to come down to join them, and to see the college.

I drove ~535 miles to get to Messiah College. It was a very nice drive, with lots of time for conversation with God. As I arrived at Messiah College, I quickly found Eric on the campus. We loaded up a few vehicles with some of his college friends, and headed off to a hunting cabin. The cabin was in a beautiful location; up a long, windy dirt road, tucked deep in the woods, near the top of a mountain. The weekend was spent in great community with great people; playing games, relaxing, eating, sharing deep spiritual conversations, hiking, praying, and quiet meditation. I even had the chance to share some of my testimony with some of Eric's friends, and they were deeply moved. Spiritually, it was a phenomenal weekend. I felt a freedom from foster care, from my dark past and childhood, from stereotypes and stigmas, and a deep joy to freely express my genuine passion and deep love for God. It was nice to be surrounded by others who were also intimately in love with Jesus! As we were all getting ready to leave, I felt God place yet another fingerprint on my life.

Before loading up the cars to return to the college campus, someone suggested we all circle up, hold hands, and just spend some time praising God and thanking Him for the great weekend. I sensed God's presence and power in a very tangible way as He, right then and there, told me that He had friends and more experiences like this for me in college. In that moment, I knew God was speaking to my heart and telling me I should attend Messiah College. He was calling for me to take a huge step of faith, to be blessed with more incredible experiences, similar to the weekend I had just shared with this group.

From a human standpoint, this made no sense. Why would I pass up a free ride to a state college in Maine, only to go to a Christian college far away that was going to cost around $100,000? This would mean that I would have to take on a debt of about $70,000 in loans! However, on the other hand, I had been certain of God's clarity in calling and directing my life when He speaks, and had been greatly blessed to obey Him.

At this time God revealed to me that my crazy, outgoing, people-loving personality could easily be misdirected at a secular state college known for its wild parties. There's a good chance I would have run to the bottle, sex, pride, and partying to escape the pain and hurt from all the abuse and trauma of my past. There were still some huge areas in my life for which I had not yet received full healing. God also knew I would find some genuine, Christ-seeking, classmates and friends at Messiah College, as well as a place for considerable healing and personal growth. Therefore, as I began my senior year of high school, I was certain where God was directing me, so I applied to only one college, Messiah College. All my eggs were in one basket!

Early in my senior year of high school, I was finally able to get my driver's license. Now I finally was able to drive. God has made me a frugal man, one who believes that we should tithe, offer, and be generous, and that we also should save up. From my savings I was able to purchase my first car, which was a baby-blue 1990 Oldsmobile Cutlass Calais, a five-gear stick-shift! An older couple had owned it, and had taken great care of it, but were getting past the point where they wanted to drive a manual vehicle. So, I was blessed to get it for a great price!

God had already, at this point in time, completely removed family from my life. By state order, Shelly and Stefan were not allowed to contact me. They also were not allowed to enter into the little town in which we lived, but they had to go to a neighboring town or city for anything they needed. However, there were more than a few times, after I had gotten my driver's license, when Shelly "happened" to be coming around the curve in the road, driving her car into the town, near where I was staying. As I saw her car approaching, as I was pulling out of the foster home, I would speed up quickly to flee from her. She would speed up and try to catch up with me, but I quickly developed a lead foot and learned how to maneuver well and get away. Praise God that He has protected me from accidents or getting too many tickets!

My senior year of high school was amazing. Although my doctors would not give the okay for me to play soccer, I was permitted to play volleyball, which I did all four years of high school. I enjoyed being active and athletic. I was also becoming aware God had placed in me an ability to connect with, influence, and lead people. During my senior year in high school, I served as the Student Council President, was involved in the drama team, helped to lead a Bible study, served with the Campus Crusade for Christ ministry, and worked hard to get senior privileges reinstated in my school—which I successfully accomplished. I also put in several hours each week working at the little town grocery store, Future Foods.

During that fall, I received a letter of acceptance from Messiah College, and I knew God was calling me to venture out on a journey that would change the entire course of my future beyond what I could ever imagine. Knowing the Potter intimately, being in the Word regularly, praying often, and fellowshipping regularly with other believers had really helped prepare me for the next great adventure on which I was about to embark! I was going to college!

Chapter 22

Off to College!

Finishing up high school was great. Doctors had assumed that I would not be able to graduate from high school, due to my head injuries, but it was actually an amazing experience, with God in the center! Graduation went well, and I was pleased that I could achieve this mile marker in life. I had exceeded expectations, and had done quite well, considering all the obstacles in the way! As my high school experience came to an end, I enjoyed what would be my last summer in Maine. I also began all the preparations to head off to college. I am not sure if I was aware that I would be moving away for good, from the state and place of incredible coldness (some people, circumstances, and the temperature), but I was very aware that God was going to be taking me on a great adventure!

My road trip to Messiah College was an important journey. It was as if God was putting yet another fingerprint on my life. God revealed to me that I was now entering a time of complete freedom to pursue Him, and that was exactly what He wanted from me. No one at college, except my good friend Eric, would know me. Therefore, this would be a situation in which I could really live out my relationship with God, without people judging me or holding my past broken family situation against me. Nor would I be any longer known as a foster child. I was excited, as I drove through all of New England down to Pennsylvania, to the campus of Messiah College, anticipating true growth and intentionality in my relationship with God.

My first semester at college was incredible. In that first semester I had my birthday and turned twenty years old. At college I was able to be me; the imperfect yet fun-loving, God-fearing young man God has made me to be, with all my faults, weaknesses, strengths, successes, ugliness, and beauty. God provided godly friends and lots of opportunities to grow in my faith and relationship with Him. My roommate was a great guy with a great spirit. He was an engineering student and became a great blessing to me.

Toward the end of my freshman year of college I was feeling a little hesitant and overwhelmed with the financial debt that I would accumulate, if I stayed at Messiah College for my full college experience. I knew God was calling me to mission work, and service and love to the hurting and needy, but I also knew that I was starting to go in a direction that would not be very lucrative or stable, at lease from the common man's perspective and understanding. After much prayer and seeking God's direction, I sensed I was supposed to continue on, trust God, and complete my education there. Shortly after I committed myself to do so, God provided yet another fingerprint on my life.

As my second semester of college was ending, I received a phone call from the financial director for the Department of Human Services in Maine. He called me and acted as though he was just checking in, but in reality, he wanted to make sure I was committed to finishing out my four years of college. Without knowing his true reason for calling, I shared with him that, though I knew I was going to be taking on a very large debt from the government in loans, I was fully committed to completing my college degree at Messiah College. He was quite pleased, and then proceeded to tell me that the state of Maine DHS had decided to evaluate my case separate from any other youth's case again. Due to the contributions I had made to help improve the state custody system, and to empower foster children to thrive, the state had decided to write me a check, payable to Messiah College, in the total amount that they had been willing to pay for me to go to a state college in Maine, as a way of encouraging me to continue my education! Praise God! It is miraculous that the secular state government would send a check to a Christian college in a state far away to help a young man. Yet again, God's hand of favor and fingerprints of love were upon me. My loan debt amount dropped from $72,000 to $50,000! Praise God!

As my first semester as a freshman in college was the time when I completed twenty years of life, and this book is specifically just about those first twenty years, I will leave the rest of the story for my next book(s). But just to catch your interest, the first semester of my sophomore year was to be spent living and studying in Israel! My next several years of life would be filled with travels, trials, hardships, healing, victory, and growth. There will come some great challenges, false accusations, great victories, and deep healing and growth. God also provides me many ridiculously amazing supernatural experiences and much travel around the earth! My plan, if it is to be God's will as well, is that I will start soon working on the second book, that shares of my life journey from 20 to 40 years old. Please continue to the next chapter of this book though, to see my final reflections about my first twenty years of life.

Chapter 23

Reflections

In closing, I want to reflect on some 'before' and 'after' pictures of my first twenty years of life. 'Before' refers to my first thirteen years of life in the abusive home situation. 'After' refers to where God has brought me to, throughout my teen years and at the end of my first twenty years of life.

In the 'before', I lived in a place with an atmosphere of intentional deceit, manipulation, depravity, physical, sexual, verbal, mental, and emotional abuse. I seldom, if ever, was told that I was loved, or experienced true love from anyone around me. It seemed to me that constantly I was told, "I hate you!" and "You are not my child." Conversations were most often filled with vulgarity and profanity. Life experiences were violent, traumatic, and depraved. My ugliness and worthlessness were highlighted by many, and I struggled with loneliness and rejection.

I was a dirty, smelly, obnoxious little kid who had no clue how to interact socially. The biological mother, Shelly, had an intentional motivation to remove pleasure from my life and punish me for being born. At an early age, I was also exposed to and encouraged to use pornography, alcohol, and cigars.

In the 'after' I had committed to a lifestyle and character of honesty. I became very transparent, like an open book. God gave me a great distaste and hatred for lies, deceit, and manipulation, because they are opposed to who God is. I was no longer under the oppression of the immense abuse. Hatred and abuse are things that God had helped to keep far from me and my heart. I had established some very good and growing relationships with friends, and was able to be healthy in sharing love with others. My words were filled with blessings, not curses, and God had been a great help and strength against profanity and vulgarity. I enjoyed bathing, showering, being clean, and was able to interact well socially. I had grown, and had gained much healing and victories over pornography and the sinful sexual influence of my first thirteen years, though God was still planning to lead me to greater depths of healing and growth in the future. I was excited to be looking forward to traveling and serving God, however and wherever He would see fit to use my life; this vessel in the hands of the Potter.

Many people would look at my 'before' and expect me to be bitter and angry. God, miraculously, has given me freedom and victory from anger and bitterness. I have always loved people, and have always felt a great satisfaction in seeing other people smiling, blessed, and succeeding. My heart has always overflowed with love for people, even in the intense and ugly abusive home situation in the 'before'. It is beyond my understanding and comprehension how someone could ever want to intentionally remove pleasure and inflict pain upon another person. God has constantly poured into my heart deep and passionate love and compassion for people. An atmosphere and environment of love is what I continue to choose!

Many people would also look at my 'before' and expect me in the 'after' to be a selfish alcoholic, a thief, bum, and/or waste of society. Praise God though, that as a JAR in the hands of the Potter, that was not, nor will it ever be who I am. I am a lover of life and of others. I am not perfect, but it is incredible to see the transforming power and hands of the Potter on my life, and where He had brought me at the end of my first twenty years of life! Only because of God's great love and intervention in my life, and His faithful, loving hands molding me, am I able to sit here today writing out and sharing with you the amazing testimony of a little jar that so greatly appreciates the hands of the Potter, who is consistently molding me for His glory! It is impossible for me to be the man of love, faith, and strength I am today without God being the center of my life. God was in the 'before' in my life, even when I was not aware He is also in the 'after' of my life. He also was, and is, in every moment in between. I am *jarr*ed and awed as I reflect back over my first twenty years of life!

I also praise God for giving me the ability to forgive the people from my past, as well as the ability to forgive myself. There is great healing and freedom in not only being able to forgive others, but also in forgiving yourself. I also desire the same for others, no matter how ugly, violent, or abusive the situation they come from, or that they cause others to experience. God can conquer the resentment, hate, and anger—and He can and wants to heal the painful wounds. However, we must let go and learn to forgive, to truly know His gift of freedom. God alone can truly change us into beautiful jars for His glory! I know this to be true because He has done it in my life! I pray continually for God to save the people from my past who have hurt me, and I pray that He will reveal His love to them! May they each be jarred into a love-relationship with the Potter!

So much took place in my first twenty years of life, and much of it will never be known by any other person other than God and me. However, I do hope that you too can see, even though I have only shared a very small portion of my first twenty years of life, just how awesome the hands of the Potter are, how constantly He placed His hands and fingerprints all over me, and throughout my first twenty years of life. Though I was not walking in an intentional love relationship with God before my accident, He was so faithful to love me, to mold and shape me, and to reveal Himself through me. He protected me and provided for me, even though I was not aware of it. His faithful fingerprints were not dependent upon me! His hands were and are all over my life!

Since Jesus Christ became my Lord, I have lived out my faith passionately, though imperfectly, wherever God has brought me. I am an intense man. Most things I do, or have ever done, I do with 110% intensity and conviction. Peter, one of Jesus' disciples, is a man I relate to well. Though he proclaimed Christ as Messiah, walked on water, and performed many miracles for God's glory, he was also a man of many shortcomings; including denying that he even knew Jesus, not once, but three times, just hours before the crucifixion. He was a man of incredible successes and incredible failures. Peter still was loved by Jesus, and used by the Potter for God's glory! Praise God for Jesus' grace and redemptive power to use us with our imperfections. I have many still. Peter was graciously restored by Jesus, and had an amazing impact on the world for God's glory! I also have been graciously restored by Jesus, and hope to have an amazing impact on the world for God's glory!

In my first twenty years of life I can see many victories for God's glory; many ways in which God has grown me and used me. I, like Peter, am a man of incredible successes and incredible failures. Even now as I write this testimony, I am aware of my weaknesses, struggles, and failures, as they are many. May the successes bring glory to God and the failures bring recognition that we are all dependent daily upon the Potter, and His great mercy, grace, and love in our lives, as He continues to mold and transform us!

Thank you for reading this book. It is my sincere desire that God has used my story to touch you in a special way. May you know what a precious vessel you are, as you remain in the marvelous hands of the Mighty Potter! Blessings, peace, and love in Jesus Christ!